The
# WILD FISH
# COOKBOOK

# The
# WILD FISH
# COOKBOOK

*Recipes from North America's*

*Top Fishing Lodges*

*Anna and David Kasabian*

With Sharon Tully

Food Photography by Glenn Scott

Food Styling by Catrine Kelty

**Creative Publishing**
**international**

www.creativepub.com

**Creative Publishing international**

Copyright © 2008
Creative Publishing international, Inc.
18705 Lake Drive East
Chanhassen, Minnesota 55317
1-800-328-3895
www.creativepub.com
All rights reserved

President/CEO: Ken Fund
Vice President Sales/Marketing: Peter Ackroyd
Publisher: Bryan Trandem
Executive Managing Editor: Barbara Harold
Production Managers: Laura Hokkanen, Linda Halls
Creative Director: Michele Lanci-Altomare
Senior Design Manager: Brad Springer
Design Managers: Jon Simpson, Mary Rohl
Additional Text: Sharon Tully
Food Photography: Glenn Scott
Food Styling: Catrine Kelty
Book Design: Peter M. Blaiwas, Vern Associates, Inc.
Cover Design: Peter M. Blaiwas, Vern Associates, Inc.

Printed in China
10 9 8 7 6 5 4 3 2 1

Library of Congress Cataloging-in-Publication Data
Kasabian, Anna.
  The Wild fish cookbook : recipes from North America's top fishing
resorts and lodges / Anna Kasabian, David Kasabian.
       p. cm.
Includes index.
  ISBN-13: 978-1-58923-317-1 (hard cover)
  ISBN-10: 1-58923-317-4 (hard cover)
  1.  Cookery (Fish) 2.  Cookery (Wild foods)  I. Kasabian, David. II.
Title.
  TX747.K27 2007
  641.6'92--dc22                                   2007007256

# Acknowledgments

Thanks to all the owners, managers, chefs, and staff members of the wonderful and unique establishments who have contributed to this cookbook.

Many, many thanks to Sharon Tully, who worked so hard to help us make this book happen—and, as usual, did a fantastic job.

Thank you to art director Peter Blaiwas of Vern Associates, Inc. Your great taste, imagination, and diligence brought the words and art into perfect harmony.

Special thanks to our photographer, Glenn Scott, and food stylist Catrine Kelty for their amazing energy and totally inspired work. For Julia Maranan and Sandra Smith, our copyeditor, thank you for all of your hard work!

Thank you to Livia Cowan, founder and president of Mariposa (www.Mariposa-gift.com), for lending us product.

And finally, thanks to our golden retriever, Amos, who sat quietly by our sides while we worked.

# Dedication

For Uncle Frank M., Charlie, Denny, and Dr. Bob—and Wally S., who always shares his catch. And for David K., who taught me to fish and tie flies. (AK)

For brother Bob and our dad, Rueben, who took us on our first fishing trips. (DK)

# Contents

# INTRODUCTION

We spent a great deal of time searching for inns, fishing camps, resorts, and ranches where fishing, the sportsman, great food, and hospitality are the ultimate focus.

One by one, as we discovered them, we invited each to contribute to this book by sharing some of their favorite recipes. The response from cooks, chefs, and owners was fabulous and, as you will soon find, so are their recipes.

It is our hope, too, that this book will introduce you to some wonderful new places to visit with your family or fishing buddies. At the back of the book, you will find a directory of all the contributors, many of which are also Orvis endorsed. Take a look, visit their websites, and perhaps you will be inspired as you plan your next fishing trip.

And when you return home, don't forget to pull this off the bookshelf! You will find a full range of recipes here, from simple to complex, from chefs and cooks all over North America—from Georgia to Alaska to British Columbia—all meant to bring you enjoyable feasts with family and friends.

—Anna and David Kasabian

# Almond-Crusted Halibut

*serves two*

Garlic powder
Onion powder
Salt and pepper
2 (6-ounce/170 g) halibut fillets
1 cup (125 g) flour, seasoned with salt
   and pepper
1 egg, whisked with a splash of milk
½ cup (65 g) slivered almonds
1 tablespoon (15 ml) olive oil
Squeeze of lemon
Fresh chopped parsley

Preheat oven to 375°F (190°C). Combine the garlic powder, onion powder, salt, and pepper, and season halibut fillets on both sides. Dredge in seasoned flour. Dip in egg wash, then press the fillets into slivered almonds so the almonds stick to the tops and bottoms. Heat the oil in a nonstick frying pan on medium-high until the oil barely smokes. Cook fillets in oiled pan until almonds are a dark golden brown. Flip fillets in the pan and transfer to the oven to finish cooking—about 5 to 8 minutes. Serve with a light squeeze of lemon and a sprinkle of parsley.

*Chef Doug Volk, Baranof Wilderness Lodge, Sitka, Alaska*

Baranof Wilderness Lodge, Sitka, Alaska

# Cajun Blackened Halibut with Papaya Chardonnay Sauce

*serves two*

2 (6-ounce/170 g) halibut fillets
Cajun spice mix
1 tablespoon (15 ml) olive oil
1 large papaya, peeled and seeded,
    cut into small dice
1 cup (235 ml) Chardonnay wine
2 tablespoons (28 g) butter
Kosher salt
White pepper
1 teaspoon (4 g) table sugar
1 teaspoon (1.25 g) fresh chopped parsley
1 teaspoon (0.33 g) fresh chopped cilantro

Preheat oven to 400°F (200°C).

Heat a medium frying pan on high. Coat fish generously with Cajun spices. Add olive oil to pan and heat until barely smoking. Place fish in pan, turn heat down to medium-high, and cook until edges are well browned. Turn over and cook bottom of fish until edges are well browned.

Keeping the juices in the first hot pan, transfer fish to an ovenproof pan and bake in oven for 5 to 8 minutes or until fish is cooked through.

Add papaya and wine to frying pan and cook until wine is reduced by half. Stir in butter, salt, pepper, sugar, parsley, and cilantro. Pour over fish.

**Chef Doug Volk, Baranof Wilderness Lodge, Sitka, Alaska**

# Cajun Salmon

*serves two*

1 pound (455 g) skinless salmon fillets
1 tablespoon (15 ml) olive oil, plus a splash
    for dressing
¼ cup (20 g) Cajun spice
1 clove garlic, minced
Salt and pepper
1 pineapple, skinned and sliced
    (or 12 rings canned, well drained)
1 onion, diced
Chopped cilantro to garnish
Splash of Champagne vinegar or
    rice wine vinegar

Preheat grill to high. Brush salmon with olive oil. Coat heavily with Cajun spice, garlic, salt, and pepper. Let salmon sit 30 minutes.

Dry pineapple thoroughly with paper towel. Brush with olive oil; season with salt and pepper. Grill pineapple until well browned. When cool, cut into 1-inch (2.5 cm) pieces. Toss with onion, cilantro, and a splash of olive oil and vinegar.

Grill salmon to desired doneness and top with pineapple mixture.

*Chef Doug Volk, Baranof Wilderness Lodge, Sitka, Alaska*

# Candied Smoked Halibut

*serves four*

6 tablespoons (180 ml) soy sauce
¾ cup (170 g) brown sugar
2 teaspoons (4 g) fresh minced ginger
½ teaspoon (1.5 g) minced garlic
½ teaspoon (1 g) ground black pepper
1½ pounds (680 g) halibut

Combine all ingredients and marinate halibut for 4 to 8 hours.

Start smoker and get temperature to approximately 110°F (50°C). Place marinated fish in smoker for 3 to 4 hours with your favorite fruit or nut wood chips. Reduce remaining marinade to a thick syrup. Gently pour small amounts of syrup over halibut every hour, maintaining temperature in smoker at approximately 110°F (43.3°C). Serve hot from the smoker.

*Chef Doug Volk, Baranof Wilderness Lodge, Sitka, Alaska*

# Halibut Lasagna

*serves eight*

3 tablespoons (42 g) butter

2 tablespoons (16 g) flour

2 cups (475 ml) milk

2 tablespoons (30 ml) lemon juice

1 tablespoon (15 ml) Worcestershire sauce

1 teaspoon (2 g) dry mustard

1 teaspoon (2.2 g) nutmeg

¼ teaspoon (0.3 g) red pepper flakes

Salt to taste

1 cup (230 g) sour cream

1 cup (115 g) shredded cheddar or
 Swiss cheese

1 tablespoon (15 ml) olive oil

1 medium onion, chopped

2 tablespoons garlic, minced

10 ounces (285 g) fresh spinach, chopped

½ teaspoon (0.35 g) dried basil leaves

15 ounces (425 g) ricotta cheese

2 eggs, beaten

12 pieces lasagna pasta, oven-ready
 or cooked

1 to 2 pounds (450 to 900 g) halibut,
 cooked and crumbled

1 cup (115 g) shredded mozzarella

¼ cup (20 g) grated Parmesan cheese

2 to 3 tablespoons (7.5 to 11 g)
 chopped parsley

½ cup (65 g) slivered almonds, toasted

Preheat oven to 375°F (190°C). In a small saucepan set on medium, heat the butter until it foams. Whisk in the flour and cook for 30 seconds. Add milk and bring to a simmer, whisking continuously. Reduce heat to low and add lemon juice, Worcestershire sauce, mustard, nutmeg, and red pepper flakes. Continue to cook, whisking often, until light and smooth (approximately 20 minutes). Mix in sour cream and cheddar or Swiss cheese and heat, while whisking, just until cheese is melted. Remove from heat.

In a medium frying pan, heat 1 tablespoon (15 ml) olive oil and cook onion and garlic until soft. Add spinach and basil and warm slightly. Remove from heat. Mix in ricotta and eggs.

Assemble in lasagna pan or a 9 x 13 x 2-inch (22.5 x 32.5 x 5 cm) casserole. Start with a third of the sauce followed by 4 pieces of pasta, half the spinach and ricotta mixture, and half the halibut. Repeat, then finish with remaining pasta, cheese sauce, mozzarella, Parmesan, and parsley. Top with almonds. Bake, uncovered, for approximately 35 minutes, until brown and bubbling. Let cool for at least 5 minutes before cutting and serving.

*Chef Jim Penrose, Baranof Wilderness Lodge, Sitka, Alaska*

# Halibut Salmon Chowder

*serves four*

½ yellow onion, diced

1½ long ribs celery, diced

1 bay leaf

½ pound (455 g) butter

½ cup (63 g) flour

2½ cups (570 ml) vegetable broth and/or combination of fish and vegetable broth

¼ pound (115 g) red potatoes, diced

½ pound (225 g) halibut, cooked and broken into bite-sized chunks

½ pound (225 g) salmon, cooked and broken into bite-sized chunks

½ tablespoon (9 g) kosher or sea salt

½ teaspoon (1 g) freshly ground black pepper

½ teaspoon (3 ml) hot red pepper sauce

Place onion, celery, bay leaf, and butter in large pot. Stir frequently until the butter melts, then add flour and stir to combine well. Turn heat to low and cook mixture for 3 to 5 minutes, stirring frequently as it thickens. Add broth and potatoes and simmer until potatoes are cooked, about 15 minutes. Remove bay leaf. Add the halibut, salmon, salt, pepper, and hot red pepper sauce. Bring to a simmer and serve.

*Chef Jim Penrose, Baranof Wilderness Lodge, Sitka, Alaska*

## Fish Doneness

- A whole fish is cooked when the thermometer (placed parallel to the dorsal fin) shows between 135° and 140°F (57° and 60°C).
- The best way to check if a fillet is cooked through is to press on top with the flat side of a knife. There should be just a little give in the flesh, and it will be translucent. Or, gently slide a thermometer into the flesh at an angle to avoid going through to the pan bottom. It should read 135° to 137°F (57° to 58°C). For less well done fish, 120°F (59°C).

# Plank-Roasted Salmon with Champagne Sauce

*serves four*

*Seasoned cedar planks (available from
   grilling and barbeque suppliers)*
*Olive oil*
*4 (6- to 8-ounce/170 to 225 g) skinless
   salmon fillets*
*2 tablespoons (15 ml) bacon drippings
   (olive oil may be substituted)*
*Salt and pepper*
*Champagne Sauce*

**Champagne Sauce**
*2 cups (470 ml) champagne
   (or white wine)*
*1 medium yellow onion, roughly chopped*
*1 tablespoon (15 ml) onion powder*
*1 cup (235 ml) heavy cream*
*1 tablespoon (15 ml) cornstarch mixed
   with 1 tablespoon (15 ml) cold water*
*Salt and pepper*

Preheat oven to 500°F (250°C). Brush seasoned cedar planks with olive oil and toast on bottom of hot oven until dark and beginning to burn. Place salmon on top. Brush salmon lightly with bacon drippings and season with salt and pepper. Place on stovetop or grill on open flames. When boards begin to smoke, place planks on bottom rack of oven. Roast to desired doneness. Serve with Champagne Sauce on the side.

In a saucepan over medium-high heat, combine champagne with onion and onion powder and heat until reduced to 1 cup (235 ml). Add cream and bring to a boil. Then add cornstarch-and-water mixture and continue heating while whisking. Season with salt and pepper. Pass through a wire strainer into a warm sauce boat or serving bowl. Discard solids.

*Baranof Wilderness Lodge, Sitka, Alaska*

# Teriyaki Salmon

*serves four*

---

1½ pounds (680 g) fresh salmon fillets,
  skinless, pin bones removed
1 cup (235 ml) soy sauce
1½ cups (340 g) brown sugar
1 tablespoon (6 g) minced fresh ginger
1 tablespoon (8 g) minced fresh garlic
1 teaspoon (2 g) ground black pepper

Combine all ingredients and marinate for 4 to 8 hours in refrigerator. Meanwhile, preheat grill to high. When very hot, clean grates thoroughly and coat with oil to help prevent sticking. Wipe excess marinade from fish. Grill fish, turning only once, until cooked through. Serve with steamed rice and stir-fried vegetables.

*Baranof Wilderness Lodge, Sitka, Alaska*

## Freezing Fish

- If you can, cook fish the day you catch it; it will never taste better.
- If you purchase fish, cook it the day you buy it, because it's already a few days old.
- Try to eat frozen fish within a month as it does not freeze as well as meat.
- If you freeze fish, make sure your freezer holds a temperature of 0°F (-18°C) or lower.

# Herb-Crusted Rainbow Trout with Sautéed Onions

*serves two*

1 15- to 18-inch (37 to 45 cm) rainbow
trout, preferably wild, gutted and scaled
1 teaspoon (6 g) kosher salt
1 teaspoon (2 g) freshly cracked black pepper
1 tablespoon (14 g) butter
1 tablespoon (15 ml) extra-virgin olive oil
2 red onions, sliced
1 handful grape tomatoes
2 cloves garlic, thinly sliced
1 cup (40 g) Marie Callender's herb-
seasoned croutons*
3 tablespoons (5 g) finely chopped fresh
rosemary
2 large eggs

Clean and rinse trout thoroughly. Leave head on for presentation. Rub salt and pepper on inside cavity of trout.

In a medium frying pan set on medium-high, add the butter and extra-virgin olive oil, onions, grape tomatoes, and garlic. Sauté until onions begin to turn golden. Remove from heat and keep warm, reserving olive oil.

Crush croutons to cornmeal consistency. Combine with rosemary.

Beat eggs and place in shallow dish large enough to accommodate fish. Coat fish with egg, then dredge in the crushed-crouton mixture.

In a very large frying pan set on medium-high, add the remaining olive oil and heat until barely smoking. Add coated fish to frying pan and cook until a golden-brown crust forms. Stuff some of the onion mixture into cavity of trout. Turn fish over and allow fish to cook until a golden-brown crust has formed and fish is cooked through.

Serve fish topped with remaining onion mixture. Serve with rice pilaf and fresh-cooked vegetables.

Wine pairing: Dom. Drouhin Oregon 2004 Chardonnay Arthur

* You may substitute plain croutons with 2 pinches each of garlic powder, basil, rosemary, oregano, and cardamom.

*Chef Trevor Walter, Big Hole C4 Lodge, Twin Bridges, Montana*

BIG HOLE C4 LODGE,
Twin Bridges, Montana

# Bacon-Wrapped Trout Stuffed with Crawfish

*serves four*

1 tablespoon (15 ml) olive oil

⅓ cup (48 g) diced onions

⅓ cup (36 g) diced celery

¼ cup (35 g) diced red pepper

¼ teaspoon (0.75 g) minced garlic

¼ pound (115 g) cleaned crawfish meat,
    fully or partially cooked

Salt and pepper to taste

⅛ cup (30 ml) white wine

¼ cup (55 g) butter

4 boned, skinless trout

6 ounces (165 g) thinly sliced
    smoked bacon

Preheat oven to 375°F (190°C). Heat olive oil in a frying pan set over medium-high heat. Sauté onion, celery, red pepper, and garlic until soft. Stir in crawfish and cook until just heated through, about 2 minutes. Season with salt and pepper. Remove mixture from pan. Reheat the pan, add wine, and scrape with a wooden spoon while cooking to dissolve all the browned bits. Add butter and let it melt. Mix with the vegetable-and-crawfish mixture and allow it to cool.

Season the trout with salt and pepper and stuff each trout with an equal amount of the cooled stuffing. Lay out bacon, sides overlapping, to length of trout (not including tail) on a piece of parchment paper. Wrap trout in bacon. Sear trout in hot pan until bacon begins to curl. Finish trout off in oven for about 6 to 8 minutes.

*Chef John Fleer, Blackberry Farm, Walland, Tennessee*

BLACKBERRY FARM, Walland, Tennessee

# Corn-Crusted Grouper with Corn Cakes

*serves four*

1 tablespoon (15 ml) olive oil
¼ cup (35 g) finely minced country ham
¼ cup (25 g) chopped green onions
3 cups (462 g) John Cope's dried corn*
½ cup (47.5 g) finely ground almonds
4 cups (430 g) dry bread crumbs
Salt and pepper
2 tablespoons (28 g) butter
4 (6-ounce/170 g) fresh grouper fillets

### Corn Cakes

¾ cup (95 g) flour
⅓ cup (40 g) cornmeal
2 tablespoons (16 g) masa harina**
¾ teaspoon (4.5 g) salt
½ teaspoon (2.5 g) baking powder
2 tablespoons (28 g) butter
¼ cup (50 g) sugar
1 egg
1 tablespoon (15 ml) molasses
1 cup (235 ml) milk
1 teaspoon (0.8 g) minced thyme

### Sauce

6 small mussels
1 shallot
½ cup (120 ml) white wine
1 cup (235 ml) vegetable stock
2 tablespoons (28 g) unsalted butter
Salt and pepper
1 tablespoon sliced sun-dried tomatoes

### Parsley Emulsion

½ bunch parsley leaves
¼ cup (60 ml) neutral-tasting oil (light
   olive oil or canola)

Preheat oven to 400°F (200°C). In a medium-sized saucepan set to medium-high, add olive oil and ham, and cook until most of the ham fat has rendered into the pan. Add green onions and cook for 1 minute or until wilted. Add dried corn, almonds, and bread crumbs. Season with salt and pepper and toss to combine. Set aside.

Heat an ovenproof frying pan on medium-high. Add the butter and then grouper into pan and top with corn mixture, approximately 4 tablespoons (25 g) per portion. Transfer pan to oven and roast approximately 5 to 7 minutes or until the grouper is cooked through.

Lower oven to 350°F (180°C). Combine flour, cornmeal, masa harina, salt, and baking powder. In a separate large bowl, cream butter and sugar together until well blended. Beat in egg and molasses. Add dry ingredients, mixing alternately with milk, until well blended. Stir in thyme. Spray 4 (4-ounce/120 ml) ramekins with nonstick spray. Divide batter among ramekins, filling until they are two thirds full. Bake for 30 to 40 minutes. Run a knife around the inside of ramekins to loosen cake. Turn ramekin upside down onto plate to un-mold.

Steam mussels with shallot and white wine. Remove mussels from shells and puree with warm vegetable stock. Return to pan to reheat. Remove from heat and whisk in butter. Season to taste with salt and pepper. Stir in sun-dried tomatoes.

Drop parsley into boiling water for 10 seconds. Drain well on paper towel. Puree and slowly trickle in oil to create an emulsion.

To serve: Place corn cake in center of plate. Place grouper on top of corn cake, crust-side up. Garnish with sauce and parsley emulsion.

*Substitute fresh corn cut from the cob and dried overnight in a
   200°F (110°C) oven.

**Available in Mexican-food section of supermarkets.

*Chef John Fleer, Blackberry Farm, Walland, Tennessee*

# Cured Trout

*serves four*

1 cup (290 g) salt
¾ cup (240 g) brown sugar
Zest of 2 lemons
2 tablespoons (13 g) anise seeds
4 trout fillets

Combine salt, brown sugar, lemon zest, and anise seeds; mix well  Line a roasting pan with parchment paper. Spread some salt mixture on top of the parchment paper. Place trout skin-side down and top with remaining salt mixture to cover completely. Place another sheet of parchment paper on top and cover with another large pan weighted with a brick. Put pans in refrigerator for 12 hours to cure trout.

Remove from refrigerator; gently scrape off excess salt using a damp towel. Serve with roasted root vegetables, salad, and crusty bread.

*Chef John Fleer, Blackberry Farm, Walland, Tennessee*

# Wild King Salmon Carpaccio with Fava Bean Horseradish Purée and Kohlrabi Basil Salad

*serves six as an appetizer*

### Salmon

*6 to 8 ounces (170 to 225 g) very fresh, high-quality salmon, trimmed*
*Garlic Yogurt (recipe follows)*
*½ cup olive oil*
*Juice of 1 lime*
*Chardonnay smoked sea salt (Regular sea salt may be substituted)*
*Fava Bean Horseradish Purée*
*Kohlrabi Basil Salad*
*Chive buds and straws for garnish*
*Chervil leaves for garnish*

### Fava Bean Horseradish Purée

*6 ounces (170 g) blanched fava beans*
*1½ tablespoons (25 ml) freshly grated horseradish*
*3 tablespoons (45 ml) vegetable stock*
*⅓ cup (80 ml) grape seed oil*

### Kohlrabi Basil Salad

*2 heads kohlrabi*
*2 basil leaves, torn or cut into ribbons*

### Garlic Yogurt

*½ cup (235 ml) plain yogurt*
*½ clove garlic, finely minced*
*4 tablespoons (60 ml) olive oil*
*Maldon sea salt to taste (or use kosher salt, if Maldon is not available)*

Pound salmon between 2 sheets of plastic wrap to roughly ⅛-inch (3 mm) thick. Trim edges to form a rectangle, if desired.

Purée beans, horseradish, and stock in blender or food processor until smooth. Drizzle in oil slowly. Strain through fine-mesh wire strainer, if desired. Reserve until ready to serve.

Peel kohlrabi and simmer in salted water until just tender but still firm. Chill for 1 hour. Coarsely grate on box grater; toss with basil and small amount of Garlic Yogurt.

Whisk together yogurt and garlic; slowly drizzle in oil. Season with Maldon salt.

To plate: Place a small amount of Garlic Yogurt on the center of each plate and lay salmon on top completely covering sauce. Brush salmon with olive oil and lime juice, season with sea salt. Place a line of fava bean purée down center of fish and top with Kohlrabi Basil Salad; garnish plate with chive buds, chive straws, and chervil leaves.

*Chef John Fleer, Blackberry Farm, Walland, Tennessee*

# Tequila Trout

*serves six*

2 tablespoons (30 ml) vegetable oil

6 (6-ounce/170 g) trout fillets

Chili powder

Lemon pepper

Dried dill

6 tablespoons (90 ml) tequila

Salsa Fresca

1 tablespoon (15 ml) chopped cilantro,
   for garnish

**Salsa Fresca**

6 ripe plum tomatoes, diced

1 onion, diced

1 jalapeño pepper, seeds and ribs removed,
   minced

2 tablespoons (8 g) chopped cilantro

1 tablespoon (15 ml) lime juice

1 tablespoon (15 ml) tequila

1 tablespoon (7 g) powdered cumin

1 tablespoon (9 g) garlic powder

1 teaspoon (6 g) salt

1 teaspoon (6 g) pepper

Heat vegetable oil in large (12-inch/30 cm) frying pan over medium-high heat until barely smoking. Sprinkle fillets with chili powder, lemon pepper, and dried dill. Add to hot pan and sauté 3 to 4 minutes or until golden brown. Flip and sauté other side for 2 minutes, or until fillets are cooked through (the flesh will flake easily when poked with a fork).

Take the pan off the burner and splash some tequila on each fillet. Ignite the tequila with a match or lighter. Shake pan gently until flames subside. Keep warm until ready to serve.

To serve, transfer cooked fillets to serving plate and top with Salsa Fresca. Garnish with fresh cilantro.

Mix all salsa ingredients well or pulse briefly in food processor for a finer texture. Make this a few hours in advance of serving.

**Chef Sue Lomperis, The Lodge and Ranch at Chama Land and Cattle Company, Chama, New Mexico**

THE LODGE AND RANCH AT CHAMA LAND
AND CATTLE COMPANY,
Chama, New Mexico

# Pan-Seared Wild Pacific Sockeye Salmon with Roasted Yam Mash and Pecan Celery Broth with Fresh Thyme

*serves four*

4 medium yams

Sea salt to taste

Coarsely ground black pepper to taste

4 (5- to 6-ounce/140 to 170 g) salmon
   fillets, skin on

1 tablespoon (15 ml) plus 1 teaspoon
   (5 ml) olive oil

4 small shallots, peeled and diced

6 cloves garlic, minced

3 stalks celery, cut into small dice

1 cup (235 ml) fish stock (vegetable stock
   can be substituted)

2 tablespoons (16 g) chopped pecans,
   toasted in a 350°F (180°C) oven for
   5 minutes

2 sprigs fresh thyme, stems removed and
   chopped

¼ cup (25 g) thinly sliced green onions for
   garnish

Preheat oven to 425°F (220°C). Bake whole yams until soft, approximately 40 minutes. When cool enough to handle, remove skin and mash with potato masher. Season with sea salt and black pepper. Keep yam mash warm.

Reduce oven temperature to 350°F (180°C). Season salmon fillets with sea salt and black pepper.

Add 1 tablespoon (15 ml) olive oil to a large frying pan set over medium-high heat. When oil is barely smoking, add salmon fillets skin-side up and sear until golden brown. Turn salmon over, transfer to a baking sheet, and place in oven to roast for approximately 5 to 6 minutes, or until salmon is done. Set aside and cover to keep warm.

Add remaining teaspoon (5 ml) olive oil to a medium-size frying pan set over medium heat. Add shallots and garlic and cook until transparent. Add celery and continue to cook. Add the fish stock and scrape the pan with a wooden spoon to dissolve all the brown bits sticking to the pan. Bring to simmer and season with salt and pepper to taste. Add chopped pecans and fresh thyme. Keep warm.

To serve, place approximately ½ to ⅓ cup (63 to 105 g) yam mash in middle of four warm soup plates. Place salmon on top of yam mash. Spoon some warm celery broth over top of cooked salmon. Garnish with sliced green onions.

*Chef Timothy May, Clayoquot Wilderness Resorts,
Tofino, British Columbia*

CLAYOQUOT WILDERNESS RESORTS,
Tofino, British Columbia

# Prosciutto-Wrapped Halibut Fillet with Spinach and Belgian Endive Salad and Red Pepper Coulis

*serves four*

4 (5- to 6-ounce/140 to 170 g)
    halibut fillets
Coarsely ground black pepper to taste
Sea salt, to taste
4 thin slices prosciutto
2 teaspoons (10 ml) olive oil, divided
3 shallots, peeled and sliced thin
6 cloves garlic, peeled and sliced
2 red peppers, cored, seeded, and diced
1 cup (235 ml) fish stock (vegetable stock
    can be substituted)
2 tablespoons (5 g) chopped fresh basil, plus
    some sprigs for garnish
2 cups (60 g) baby spinach, washed
    and dried
6 leaves Belgian endive, sliced into
    matchsticks

Preheat oven to 350°F (180°C). Season halibut fillets with coarsely ground black pepper and a pinch of sea salt. Wrap prosciutto around halibut. Heat 1 teaspoon (5 ml) olive oil in a large frying pan until barely smoking. Sear one side of prosciutto-wrapped halibut until golden brown. Turn halibut over, transfer to a baking sheet, and cook in the oven for approximately 6 to 8 minutes, or until the halibut is cooked through. Set aside and keep warm.

Heat remaining 1 teaspoon (5 ml) olive oil in a small frying pan and sauté shallots and garlic until transparent. Add red peppers and cook, covered, for 2 minutes. Try not to get any color on the peppers.

Add fish stock, bring to a simmer, and season to taste. Remove and drain red pepper once it is soft. In a blender, puree red pepper, using some stock as needed to thin coulis. Add fresh basil. Keep warm.

Mix spinach and Belgian endive in a bowl. Divide into four portions. Season lightly with salt and pepper.

Place salad on soup plate and top with halibut. Drizzle red pepper coulis over top. Garnish with basil sprigs.

***Chef Timothy May, Clayoquot Wilderness Resorts, Tofino, British Columbia***

# Bass with Leek Sauce

*serves four*

4 (6- to 7-ounce/170 to 200 g) bass fillets,
    skin on
Salt and pepper
1 tablespoon (15 ml) plus 1 teaspoon
    5 ml) vegetable oil
2 shallots, peeled and minced
3 leeks (white part only), thinly sliced
½ cup (120 ml) chicken stock
Squeeze of lemon juice
2 tablespoons sliced fresh chives

Preheat oven to 400°F (200°C). Season bass with salt and pepper. Heat large frying pan over medium-high heat. Add 1 tablespoon (15 ml) vegetable oil. When oil just begins to smoke, add fillets and sear until light golden. Transfer fillets to baking sheet and finish cooking in oven for about 7 minutes, or until just cooked through.

Heat a large saucepan over medium-high heat. Add the remaining 1 teaspoon (5 ml) vegetable oil and sauté shallots and leeks until translucent, about 5 minutes. Do not allow to brown.  Add chicken stock, cover pan, and simmer until leeks are very tender, about 15 minutes. Transfer to blender and puree mixture until smooth. Strain through fine strainer, if desired. Season with lemon juice, salt, and pepper, and keep warm.

Serve bass fillets with Leek Sauce and garnish with chives.

*Chef Noelle Wright, Clearwater Lodge on The Pitt River, Fall River Mills, California*

CLEARWATER LODGE,
*Fall River Mills, California*

# Cornmeal-Crusted Catfish with Corn and Black Bean Salsa

*serves six*

2 ears corn, husked

1 cup (170 g) cooked black beans, rinsed
 and drained

½ cup (55 g) peeled, seeded, and diced
 tomatoes

1 small jalapeño, seeded and chopped

1 cucumber, chopped

⅓ cup (48 g) minced red onion

⅓ cup (45 g) diced red bell pepper

¼ cup (60 ml) chopped cilantro

¼ cup (60 ml) lime juice

1 teaspoon (6 g) kosher salt

¼ teaspoon (0.5 g) freshly ground black
 pepper

¼ cup (60 ml) olive oil

6 (5- to 6-ounce/140 to 170 g)
 catfish fillets

½ cup (120 ml) buttermilk

1 cup (140 g) cornmeal

Preheat grill to high. Grill corn, rotating every few minutes, until slightly charred and cooked, about 10 minutes total. Cool and cut kernels from cobs.

In a bowl, combine corn, black beans, tomatoes, jalapeño, cucumber, red onion, red pepper, cilantro, and lime juice. Season to taste with salt and pepper. Chill up to 8 hours, but return to room temperature before serving.

Preheat oven to 400°F (200°C). Heat oil in large skillet over medium-high heat until barely smoking. Season fillets with salt and pepper. Dip fillets in buttermilk and dredge in cornmeal. Sauté fish in hot oil until browned, about 2 to 3 minutes per side. Transfer to baking sheet and finish in oven for 3 to 4 minutes. Serve hot with salsa on side.

*Chef Noelle Wright, Clearwater Lodge on The Pitt River, Fall River Mills, California*

# Smoked Trout Cakes

*makes sixteen appetizer-sized cakes*

*4 large baking potatoes*

*3 large eggs, lightly beaten*

*4 tablespoons (55 g) unsalted butter, melted*

*½ cup (50 g) coarsely chopped chives or green onions*

*¼ cup (15 g) finely chopped flat-leaf (Italian) parsley*

*½ teaspoon (1.5 g) salt*

*¼ teaspoon (0.5 g) freshly ground pepper*

*1 pound (450 g) skinless, boneless smoked trout, flaked*

*2 cups (220 g) panko (Japanese bread crumbs)*

*Canola oil, for frying*

*Lemon wedges*

*Horseradish Cream*

*1 cup (230 g) sour cream*

*¼ cup (27.5 g) freshly grated horseradish*

*1 tablespoon (15 ml) freshly squeezed lemon juice*

*Salt and pepper to taste*

Preheat oven to 400°F (200°C). Bake potatoes for about 45 minutes or until tender. Let cool slightly, then halve potatoes and scoop insides into large bowl. Discard skins. Mash potatoes, then add eggs, butter, chives or green onions, parsley, salt, and pepper, and combine well. Gently fold in trout and shape mixture into 16 small patties, about ½ cup (105 g) each.

Lower oven to 350°F (180°C). Spread panko bread crumbs on plate and lightly dredge fish cakes. The cakes may then be refrigerated for up to 2 hours before frying.

In large skillet, heat ¼ inch (0.6 cm) canola oil until barely smoking. Fry fish cakes in batches over moderately high heat until browned and crisp, about 2 minutes. Turn fish cakes, lower heat to medium, and cook until browned on bottom, about 2 minutes more. Transfer to baking sheet and bake for 7 to 8 minutes or until heated through.

Whisk all ingredients for horseradish cream together.

Serve trout cakes with horseradish cream and lemon wedges.

*Chef Noelle Wright, Clearwater Lodge on The Pitt River, Fall River Mills, California*

# Salmon with Mustard-Caper Sauce

*serves four*

4 (6- to 7-ounce/170 to 200 g)
    *salmon fillets*
2 tablespoons (28 ml) soy sauce
4 cloves garlic, sliced thin lengthwise,
    divided
1 teaspoon (5 ml) olive oil, divided
1 red bell pepper, peeled, cored, and diced
2 tablespoons (30 ml) plus 2 teaspoons
    10 ml) dry white wine
¾ cup (175 ml) heavy cream
2 tablespoons (30 g) Dijon mustard
2 tablespoons (17 g) plus two teaspoons
    (5 g) capers, rinsed and drained
2 tablespoons (8 g) minced fresh parsley
Salt and freshly ground black pepper
    to taste
Lemon slices

Rub salmon with soy sauce and half of the garlic and marinate in refrigerator for 1 hour.

Preheat oven to 400°F (200°C).

Heat a medium-sized frying pan over medium heat. Add ½ teaspoon (2.5 ml) olive oil and sauté remaining garlic until golden. Do not burn. Discard garlic. Add red pepper, cover, and cook over low heat until very tender, about 5 minutes. Add wine and reduce by half. Add heavy cream and simmer until thickened. Stir in mustard, capers, and parsley. Season to taste with salt and pepper. Keep sauce warm.

Heat a large nonstick pan over medium-high heat. Add remaining ½ teaspoon (2.5 ml) olive oil and heat until barely smoking. Sear salmon on one side until golden brown. Turn the fillets over, transfer to a baking sheet, and bake for about 6 to 8 minutes, or until just cooked through. Serve with sauce and lemon slices.

**Chef Noelle Wright, Clearwater Lodge on The Pitt River, Fall River Mills, California**

# Plank-Roasted Wild Salmon with Cider-Brandy Glaze

*serves four*

4 (6-ounce/170 g) fillets wild salmon,
   skinned and deboned

Salt and pepper

2 cups (475 ml) apple cider

½ cup (120 ml) honey

2 ounces (60 ml) brandy

2 tablespoons (30 ml) olive oil

1 tablespoon (14 g) butter

Preheat oven to 400°F (200°C). Preheat cedar planks for approximately 10 minutes before using them. Season both sides of salmon liberally with salt and pepper.

In a small saucepan, combine cider, honey, and brandy over medium-high heat and reduce by two thirds. The resulting glaze should be about the consistency of maple syrup or a bit thinner. Place olive oil and butter in a large nonstick skillet over medium-high heat. When butter stops foaming, place salmon skin-side up in pan and sear for about 3 minutes or until golden brown. Flip and sear for approximately 1 minute more. Remove from pan and place on preheated cedar plank. Brush each piece of salmon liberally with glaze. Place in oven and bake for about 5 to 7 minutes or until the salmon is cooked properly. Wild salmon is best when just a touch over medium rare. Remove salmon from oven and brush liberally again with glaze just before serving.

Wine suggestions: A buttery California Chardonnay or a floral white with some weight, such as Viognier.

*Chef Tim Cabradilla, Crescent H Ranch in Jackson Hole, Wilson, Wyoming*

CRESCENT H RANCH IN JACKSON HOLE,
Wilson, Wyoming

# Boursin, Roasted Pepper, and Spinach-Stuffed Rainbow Trout

*serves four*

4 (10-ounce/280 g) rainbow trout, butterflied, heads and pin bones removed

*Salt and pepper*

1 (5.2-ounce/147 g) package Boursin or other herbed soft cheese, removed from aluminum casing and left at room temperature to soften slightly

½ cup (67.5 g) roasted red peppers, cut into thin strips

2 cups (60 g) baby spinach leaves, washed and dried

3 tablespoons (45 ml) olive oil

1 tablespoon (14 g) butter

Preheat oven to 350°F (180°C). Season the cavity inside each trout with salt and pepper.

Combine Boursin, red peppers, and spinach in a bowl. Season to taste with salt and pepper. Mix thoroughly. Place one fourth of stuffing inside each trout. Carefully fold one side of trout over the other, encasing stuffing between the two halves.

Place olive oil and butter in a large nonstick frying pan over medium-high heat. When butter stops foaming, place trout in pan skin-side down. Sear for about 4 minutes or until skin becomes crisp. Flip trout and crisp other side as well.

Remove trout from skillet and place on a greased or nonstick baking sheet. Bake for about 8 to 10 minutes or until cooked through.

Wine suggestions: White Burgundy, Sancerre, or a well-oaked Chardonnay from Napa

**Chef Tim Cabradilla, Crescent H Ranch in Jackson Hole, Wilson, Wyoming**

# Cedar-Planked Salmon

*serves two*

1 tablespoon (15 ml) extra-virgin olive oil
2 (6-ounce/170 g) salmon fillets
1 small shallot, minced
1 clove garlic, minced
1 tablespoon (14 g) butter
2 teaspoons (5 g) flour
¼ cup (60 ml) white wine
¼ cup (60 ml) lemon juice
¼ cup (60 ml) orange juice
Parsley for garnish

*Special equipment:* Cedar plank, available from barbeque and grill stores. Do not use cedar shingles from the lumber store. Submerge plank in water and soak for 4 hours. Place something heavy, such as a can from the cupboard, on top of the plank to hold it under water.

Preheat oven to 350°F (190°C). Heat the olive oil in a frying pan until barely smoking. Sear fillets for 2 minutes each side. Place fillets on cedar plank and bake in oven for 10 minutes or until cooked through.

Using the same frying pan and oil, sauté shallot and garlic until soft. Add butter and flour. Mix thoroughly. Add wine, lemon juice, and orange juice. Simmer for a few minutes until the sauce thickens a bit. To serve, pour sauce over salmon and garnish with parsley.

**Eldred Preserve, Eldred, New York**

ELDRED PRESERVE, Eldred, New York

# Crab-Stuffed Trout

*serves six*

1½ cups (200 g) cooked crabmeat

tablespoon (10 g) minced onion

1 tablespoon (7.5 g) minced celery

1 tablespoon (5 g) minced white
   mushrooms

2 teaspoons (10 ml) lemon juice

2 teaspoons (10 ml) Worcestershire sauce

1 teaspoon (6 g) salt

2 dashes hot red pepper sauce

Dash black pepper

Dash cayenne pepper

1 tablespoon (3.8 g) chopped parsley

2 tablespoons (14 g) bread crumbs

½ cup (120 ml) milk

1 whole egg

6 whole trout, gutted and scaled

6 tablespoons (84 g) butter, melted, divided

Paprika as needed

1 tablespoon (4 g) minced parsley

Preheat oven to 425°F (220°C). Carefully inspect crabmeat by hand and remove any remaining shell or cartilage. Shred crabmeat by hand. Combine crab and next 13 ingredients, through egg. Stir gently to combine. Refrigerate for 1 to 2 hours.

Gently fill the cavity inside each trout with one sixth of the stuffing and push the trout closed. Brush both sides of trout with half the melted butter. Place on baking sheet. Bake 20 to 25 minutes or until skin is brown and crisp and the center of the stuffing reaches a temperature of 145°F (63°C) when tested with an instant-read thermometer, about 20 minutes. Sprinkle with paprika and parsley and drizzle remaining melted butter on trout before serving.

**Eldred Preserve, Eldred, New York**

# Spring Trout

*serves two*

Flour for dredging

Salt and pepper

2 fresh (10- to 12- ounce/280 to 340 g)
   trout, gutted, scaled, deboned, and
   butterflied

2 tablespoons (28 g) butter, divided

¼ cup (38 g) diced fresh tomato

1 tablespoon (10 g) chopped leeks

1 tablespoon (10 g) capers, drained
   and rinsed

Splash of white wine

Juice of 1 lemon

Parsley for garnish

Season flour with salt and pepper. Dredge trout in seasoned flour. Heat 1 tablespoon (14 g) butter in nonstick frying pan set over medium-high heat. Sauté trout, flesh-side down, for 2 minutes. Flip the fish over in the pan and sauté for additional 2 minutes on skin side. Transfer fish to serving dish and cover loosely with foil to keep warm until ready to serve.

Return frying pan to medium-high heat. Add tomato, leeks, and capers. Sauté for 1 minute and then add remaining butter, white wine and lemon juice. Cook until reduced by half. Pour over over trout, head to tail. Garnish with chopped parsley.

**Eldred Preserve, Eldred, New York**

# Sunrise Trout

*serves four*

---

2 to 4 (10- to 12-ounce/280 to 340 g)
  *whole trout, gutted and scaled*
¼ cup (60 ml) butter, melted
*Salt and pepper*
1 cup (108 g) bread crumbs
¼ cup (60 ml) white wine
1 tablespoon (4 g) chopped parsley
1 lemon, juiced
*Lemon wedges for garnish*
*Parsley sprigs for garnish*

Preheat oven to 375°F (190°C). Brush trout with melted butter, then season with salt and pepper. Roll in bread crumbs to coat. Place on rimmed baking sheet pan and bake for 20 minutes. Remove trout and add white wine, parsley, and lemon juice. Shake baking sheet over medium flame on top of stove while scraping with a wooden spoon to dissolve all the brown bits in the pan. Reduce by half. Add remaining melted butter to baking sheet and season with salt and pepper. Drizzle over trout and garnish with lemon wedges and sprigs of parsley.

**Eldred Preserve, Eldred, New York**

## Baking Fish

- *You can bake a whole fish in a porcelain gratin-style dish and serve it in that as well. If you don't have one, cook it in a sheet pan and transfer it to a platter for serving.*
- *A good rule of thumb for baking a whole fish is 400° to 450°F (200° to 230°C); the smaller the fish, the hotter the oven. Figure a whole fish takes 15 minutes per inch of thickness; gauge at the base of the head where it's the thickest.*

# Trout Grenoble

*serves four*

2 tablespoons (30 ml) vegetable oil
    for frying
4 whole trout, gutted and scaled
Salt and pepper
1 cup (125 g) flour for dredging
6 canned artichoke hearts, drained and
    quartered
1 large tomato, diced
1 small green pepper, stemmed, cored, and
    diced
2 tablespoons (18 g) capers, washed and
    drained
Juice of 1 lemon
¼ cup (60 ml) dry white wine
2 tablespoons (28 g) cold butter

In a frying pan set on medium-high, heat oil until barely smoking. Season trout with salt and pepper and dredge in flour. Fry each side of the trout until golden and remove to platter. Discard oil from frying pan and add all remaining ingredients except butter. Bring to a boil in pan and swirl in butter until it disappears. Season and spoon sauce over trout to serve.

**Eldred Preserve, Eldred, New York**

# Trout Newburg

*serves four*

8 trout fillets
Salt and pepper
Flour for dredging, plus 2 tablespoons (15 g)
5 tablespoons (70 g) butter
½ pound (225 g) peeled and
    deveined shrimp
¼ cup (60 ml) dry sherry
1 cup (235 ml) heavy cream
1 tablespoon (7 g) paprika
1 tablespoon (4 g) chopped parsley

Season trout fillets with salt and pepper and dredge in flour.

Heat butter in a frying pan set on medium heat. When the butter stops sizzling, add trout. Do not crowd. Cook in batches, unless you have an especially large pan that can accommodate all eight fillets. Sauté trout 2 to 3 minutes on each side. If butter starts to burn, wipe out the pan and start over with fresh butter. Transfer trout to a platter and keep warm.

Add shrimp to pan and cook for 5 minutes, stirring occasionally. Stir in 2 tablespoons (16 g) flour. Add sherry, cream, and paprika. Bring to a simmer and whisk constantly until thickened, about 3 minutes. Season with salt and pepper and spoon over trout fillets. Garnish with parsley. Serve with crusty bread.

*Eldred Preserve, Eldred, New York*

# Grilled Wild Salmon with Maple-Ginger Marinade

*serves two*

1 teaspoon (2 g) crushed fennel seed
1 tablespoon (8 g) minced fresh garlic
2 tablespoons (6 g) minced fresh ginger
1 teaspoon (6 g) fine sea salt
1 teaspoon (2 g) cracked black pepper
¼ cup (120 ml) real maple syrup
¼ cup (120 ml) olive oil
2 pounds (900 g) wild salmon fillets

Combine all ingredients, except salmon, in large bowl. Add salmon to mixture and marinate for approximately 1 hour. Preheat grill to high. Grill salmon fillets until preferred doneness, about 5 minutes per side, while basting fish with remaining marinade. Grill cover should be down in order for marinade to set properly on fish.

*Elk Lake Lodge, North Hudson, New York*

ELK LAKE LODGE,
North Hudson, New York

# Trout with Wild Mushroom and Leek Stuffing

*serves four*

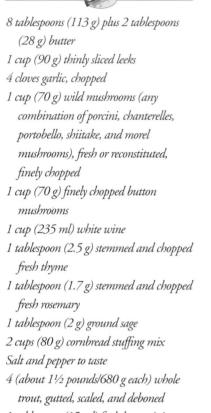

8 tablespoons (113 g) plus 2 tablespoons
 (28 g) butter

1 cup (90 g) thinly sliced leeks

4 cloves garlic, chopped

1 cup (70 g) wild mushrooms (any
 combination of porcini, chanterelles,
 portobello, shiitake, and morel
 mushrooms), fresh or reconstituted,
 finely chopped

1 cup (70 g) finely chopped button
 mushrooms

1 cup (235 ml) white wine

1 tablespoon (2.5 g) stemmed and chopped
 fresh thyme

1 tablespoon (1.7 g) stemmed and chopped
 fresh rosemary

1 tablespoon (2 g) ground sage

2 cups (80 g) cornbread stuffing mix

Salt and pepper to taste

4 (about 1½ pounds/680 g each) whole
 trout, gutted, scaled, and deboned

1 tablespoon (15 ml) fresh lemon juice

Preheat oven to 350°F (180°C). Melt 8 tablespoons (113 g) of butter in large heavy skillet over medium heat.

Add leeks, garlic, wild mushrooms, and button mushrooms and sauté for 10 minutes. Add wine, thyme, rosemary, and sage and cook for another 5 minutes (or until most of the liquid is evaporated).

Add cornbread stuffing mix to above mixture and fold until evenly distributed.  Add salt and pepper to taste.

Stuff each fish generously with stuffing mixture. Melt remaining 2 tablespoons (28 g) of butter and combine with lemon juice. Brush each fish liberally with lemon mixture. Bake for about 20 minutes or until stuffing is heated through.

*Elk Lake Lodge, North Hudson, New York*

# Blackened Salmon

*serves two*

2 (8-ounce/226 g) salmon fillets, skin on
2 tablespoons (30 ml) olive oil
¼ cup (28 g) Cajun spice seasoning
6 tablespoons (85 g) butter, melted
Juice of 1 fresh lemon
2 tablespoons (17.2 g) capers
2 teaspoons (2 g) chopped chives

Preheat oven to 350° F (180 ° C). Heat a cast-iron skillet or grill pan on high heat until it starts to smoke. Pat salmon fillets dry with paper towels. Coat liberally with olive oil and sprinkle Cajun seasoning evenly on flesh side. Place fish flesh-side down on hot skillet. Let sizzle and smoke for 3 to 4 minutes. Turn fish over in pan and place in oven for 4 to 5 minutes. Flesh should be just slightly pink inside. Garnish with melted butter and lemon juice on serving plate. Sprinkle with capers and chives and serve.

*Chef Pierre Coutou, Favorite Bay Lodge, Angoon, Alaska*

FAVORITE BAY LODGE,
Angoon, Alaska

# Halibut Ceviche

*serves four*

2 pounds (900 g) halibut fillet, cut into
½-inch (1 cm) cubes
2 jalapeño chilies, seeded and finely
    chopped (use 1 for less heat)
2 limes, juiced
½ cup (8 g) chopped cilantro
½ cup (64 g) carrots cut into small dice
½ cup (80 g) diced red onion
2 ounces (60 ml) Bloody Mary mix
Dash hot red pepper sauce
Salt and pepper to taste
Diced avocado, optional

Combine all ingredients except avocado in a large bowl and mix gently by hand. Refrigerate overnight. Serve with deep-fried flour tortilla chips.

Optional: Add diced avocado just before serving.

*Chef Pierre Coutou, Favorite Bay Lodge, Angoon, Alaska*

## How Do You Know Your Fish is Fresh?

If you purchase your fish, here are a few things to look for to make sure it's fresh:

- *Fresh ocean or freshwater fish smells very pleasant. Ocean fish should smell of seaweed, and freshwater fish should smell of waterweeds. A good fish store will allow a customer to lift the gill for a quick whiff.*
- *The body of the fish should be glossy; the flesh firm and elastic. Flesh colors should be metallic and iridescent. Scales should be shiny, tight, and damp and covered with a light transparent mucus. Press your finger into the side of the flesh; there should be no imprint left! Note: If you can, buy a fish whole as it is easier to tell if it is fresh.*
- *Clear, bulging eyes.*
- *Damp, bright red gills.*
- *Guts smooth and clean.*
- *Tail should be flat.*
- *The belly wall of a gutted fish should be very pale, and the backbone should be adhered to the flesh. Dark red or brown belly flesh should be avoided.*
- *For steaks and fillets, the surface should be moist; no film; slightly translucent, not opaque; no spaces in the flake.*

# Crispy Whole Fish with Szechuan Glaze

*serves four*

*Vegetable oil for deep-frying*

*1 (2- to 3-pound/ 900 to 1360 g) whole rockfish, sea bass, or other firm, white-fleshed fish, gutted and scaled*

*½ cup (62 g) all-purpose flour*

*½ cup (64 g) cornstarch*

*½ cup (55 g) shredded carrots*

*½ cup (50 g) julienned green onions*

*½ cup (35 g) sliced shiitake mushrooms*

*½ cup (46 g) sliced red and yellow peppers*

*¼ cup (26 g) bean sprouts*

*½ cup (49 g) julienned snap peas*

*¼ cup (25g) chopped peanuts*

### Szechuan Glaze

*1 cup (235 ml) hoisin sauce*

*1 tablespoon (8.5 g) minced garlic*

*1 tablespoon (6 g) minced ginger*

*2 tablespoons (28 ml) honey*

*2 tablespoons (28 ml) Asian sweet chili sauce*

Pour cooking oil into a very large, deep pan to a depth of 3 inches (7.5 cm), taking care that it is less than one half the depth of the pan. Heat cooking oil to 325°F (170°C).

Make deep crisscross cuts on the skin of both sides of fish. Mix flour and cornstarch and dredge fish thoroughly in mixture. Completely submerge whole fish in 325°F (170°C) cooking oil for approximately 12 minutes, or until crispy and golden brown. Drain well and plate immediately. Top fish with sliced vegetables.

Combine all glaze ingredients in a small saucepan and bring sauce to medium heat. Drizzle Szechuan Glaze over fish and sliced vegetables. Sprinkle chopped peanuts over sauce and serve family-style.

*Chef Pierre Coutou, Favorite Bay Lodge, Angoon, Alaska*

# Horseradish-Encrusted Chinook Salmon with Garlic-Thyme Buerre Blanc

*serves six*

2 teaspoons (10 ml) olive oil

2 cloves garlic, finely chopped

2 tablespoons (28 ml) Pernod or other
   anise-flavored liqueur, if desired

3 cups (700 ml) white wine

1 cup (235 ml) heavy cream

½ pound (225 g) butter, cubed

1 tablespoon (2.5 g) thyme, freshly chopped
   or 1 teaspoon (1.5 g) dried thyme

Salt and pepper to taste


6 (6- to 8 ounce/170 to 225 g) fillets fresh
   skinless Chinook salmon

1 tablespoon (15 ml) olive or canola oil

2 ounces (55 g) prepared horseradish

½ cup (60 g) panko (Japanese bread
   crumbs)

Preheat oven to 450°F (230°C). In a medium saucepan over medium-high heat, add olive oil and garlic. Sauté until garlic becomes translucent but before it turns golden. Add the Pernod and white wine. (If using dried thyme, add it when the wine is added.) Reduce by three fourths. Add heavy cream and simmer until sauce thickens and coats the back of a spoon. Remove pan from heat. Whisk in butter cubes a couple at a time. Keep whisking so the sauce doesn't break. Add fresh thyme, then salt and pepper to taste. Store sauce in warm, but not hot, place, until ready to serve.

Season the fillets with salt and pepper. Heat the oil in a large frying pan until the oil is barely smoking. Add the fillets and cook until the first side is golden brown. Turn the fillets over in the pan and cook the second side until golden brown and the salmon is medium-rare. Remove from heat and transfer fillets to a greased baking sheet.

Spread horseradish over salmon (the more you use, the spicier it will be). Sprinkle panko over each fillet, coating the horseradish. Bake until panko turns golden brown and the salmon is cooked through. Serve with buerre blanc drizzled in a pool around salmon.

Parmesan risotto or herbed wild rice makes a nice accompaniment.

*Chef Matthew Currey, Flying B Ranch, Kamiah, Idaho*

FLYING B RANCH,
Kamiah, Idaho

# Grilled Steelhead Trout with Tomato-Herb Sauce

*serves four*

*1 small yellow onion, julienned*

*1 tablespoon (10 g) minced garlic*

*½ cup (120 ml) gin*

*24 ounces (720 ml) V8 or other
  vegetable juice*

*¼ ounce (7 g) dried juniper berries,
  wrapped in cheesecloth*

*½ ounce (15 g) mixed fresh herbs
  (rosemary, basil, thyme), chopped*

*2 tablespoons (28 g) unsalted butter*

*Salt and pepper to taste*

*Olive oil*

*8 (6- to 8-ounce/170 to 225 g)
  steelhead fillets*

Sauté onion and garlic in medium saucepan on medium-high heat until they begin to caramelize. Deglaze pan with gin (be careful of flame). Once flames subside, add vegetable juice and juniper berries. Let simmer over low heat for 35 to 40 minutes. Stir occasionally.

Once sauce has reduced and thickened, remove from heat. Remove juniper berries and place remaining sauce (there should be approximately 2 cups [470ml]) in blender. Blend in fresh herbs, then slowly add butter. Season with salt and pepper to taste. Keep warm until ready to use. Leftover sauce can be refrigerated for up to a week and reheated before use.

Preheat grill to high. Season fish and rub with oil to prevent sticking to grill. Place fish on hot grill and cook to desired doneness. To serve, place on plate and drizzle with sauce. Risotto or wild rice is a great accompaniment.

Wine pairing: A full-bodied Chardonnay or Pinot Noir.

**Chef Michael Currey, Flying B Ranch, Kamiah, Idaho**

# Tequila-Lime Cutthroat Trout with Sun-Dried Tomato Salad

*serves six*

6 fresh cutthroat trout, gutted, scaled, deboned, heads and tails removed

Salt and pepper

4 tablespoons (56 g) butter, divided

4 ounces (120 ml) tequila, divided

Juice of 2 limes, divided

4 ounces (115 g) sun-dried tomatoes (not packed in oil), cut into thin sticks and rehydrated by soaking in warm water

1 (8- to 10-ounce/226 to 280 g) package fresh baby spinach

1 small red onion, finely chopped

1 red pepper, roasted, skinned, and julienned (jarred may be substituted)

1 bunch cilantro, washed and roughly chopped

1 (14-ounce/395 g) can artichoke hearts, drained and quartered

½ cup (50 g) kalamata olives, pitted and sliced

1 cup (235 ml) rice wine vinegar

¼ cup (60 ml) olive oil

4 ounces (115 g) feta cheese

 Season trout, inside and out, with salt and pepper. Place 2 tablespoons (28 g) butter in 12-inch (30 cm) nonstick frying pan set over medium-high heat, swirling until butter is melted and bubbling. Sear 3 of the trout skin-side up for 1 minute. Add 2 ounces (60 ml) tequila, watching out for any flames. Return pan to heat. Add the juice of 1 lime and cook until liquid evaporates. Flip trout and sear skin-side down until fish is done, about 1 minute more.

Remove cooked trout from pan, wipe pan out with a paper towel, and repeat with the remaining 3 trout. (Cooked trout can be placed in warm oven until ready to serve.)

Toss tomatoes, spinach, onion, red pepper, cilantro, artichokes, and olives together. Add vinegar, oil, salt, and pepper to taste.

To serve, place salad on plate and lay trout on top. Crumble feta cheese over trout.

Moroccan couscous makes a nice accompaniment.

*Chef Michael Currey, Flying B Ranch, Kamiah, Idaho*

# Trout with Almonds

*serves four*

4 whole trout, gutted and scaled
Freshly cracked black peppercorns
Juice of 1 lemon, divided
6 tablespoons (85 g) butter
2 tablespoons (30 ml) oil
½ cup (65 g) sliced almonds
Parsley, minced
Lemon slices

Preheat oven to 200°F (110°C). Rub trout with pepper and a few drops of lemon juice. Warm serving platter in oven. In a very large frying pan, melt 2 tablespoons butter (28 g) with the oil over medium-high heat. Sauté trout on one side until lightly browned (approximately 3 to 5 minutes), then turn fish and continue cooking. Trout is done when it flakes at the touch of a fork. Remove fish to warm platter and wipe out pan. Melt remaining 4 tablespoons (56 g) butter. Sauté almonds until golden. Add remaining lemon juice and parsley to almonds in pan. Swirl and pour over trout. Garnish with lemon slices.

**Gaston's White River Resort, Lakeview, Arkansas**

GASTON'S WHITE RIVER RESORT
Lakeview, Arkansas

# White River Fried Trout

*serves six*

2 eggs

2 cups (250 g) flour

Salt and freshly ground black pepper

12 boneless trout fillets

½ cup (120 ml) olive oil

8 tablespoons (115 g) butter

½ small onion, chopped (optional)

1 clove garlic, chopped (optional)

2 hard-boiled eggs, shelled and sliced

Watercress or parsley (for garnish)

Preheat oven to 350°F (180°C). Cracks eggs into a bowl and whisk for a few seconds. Mix flour and a generous amount of salt and pepper in another bowl. Place trout fillets in egg mixture, then dredge in flour. Repeat for all 12 fillets.

Place oil and butter in a large frying pan and heat until butter stops foaming. If butter starts to burn, decrease heat. Place coated fillets in pan and cook for approximately 5 minutes, until golden brown. Turn fish, adding chopped onion and/or garlic if desired, and continue cooking about 5 minutes, until second side is golden brown. Transfer to baking sheet and bake in oven for 10 to 15 minutes. Allow fish to rest for 5 minutes after removing from oven. Garnish with hard-boiled egg slices and watercress or parsley.

**Gaston's White River Resort, Lakeview, Arkansas**

# Gravlax

*serves twelve to sixteen as an appetizer*

2 whole salmon fillets, scaled and boned
½ cup (120 ml) vodka
1 cup (290 g) coarse kosher salt, or as needed
2 cups (290 g) brown sugar, or as needed
⅓ cup (16 g) dried dill or 6 large sprigs
    fresh dill
Coarsely ground black pepper

Scratch skin side of fillets with top of sharp knife (do not cut through skin) to allow moisture to seep through skin during curing process. Lay one fillet skin-side down on a flat surface and brush on vodka. Sprinkle with just enough salt to cover the flesh. Using your hands, cover entire flesh surface of salmon and salt with ½-inch (1.25 cm) layer of brown sugar. Add heavy sprinkling of dill and pepper.

Repeat salting process with remaining fillet and quickly flip onto the first fillet, flesh side onto the brown sugar coating. Wrap both fillets tightly with plastic wrap and place on a rimmed sheet pan large enough for fillets to lie flat. Place wood plank or weight on top of fillets and refrigerate. Remove every 12 hours to drain liquid from baking sheet and flip salmon over (so upper fillet is now on bottom). Continue process for 2 to 3 days, depending on how cured you like the salmon.

Remove wrap, rinse, and pat dry. Then let salmon air dry in refrigerator for at least 8 hours. (Note: the fish aroma might be picked up by other foods in the refrigerator.)

To serve, lay fillets flesh-side up on dry pan and place in freezer for 2 to 3 hours, until salmon is firm and just starting to freeze. Thin slice on bias while fish is firm. Fillets can be vacuum-packed and frozen for up to 1 year or kept in refrigerator for 1 to 2 weeks.

*Executive Chef Scott Wells, Great Alaska*
*Adventure Lodge, Sterling, Alaska*

GREAT ALASKA ADVENTURE LODGE,
Sterling, Alaska

# Warm Artichoke and Smoked Salmon Dip

*serves eight to twelve as an appetizer*

*1 each small red, yellow, and green bell
pepper, cut into ½-inch (1.25 cm) dice*

*1 small red onion, cut into ½- inch
(1.25 cm) dice*

*Olive oil , to coat*

*2 cups canned artichoke hearts (not
marinated)*

*½ cup (68 g) smoked salmon, coarsely
chopped*

*1 (8-ounce/230 g) package cream cheese,
softened and cut into large cubes*

*4 dashes hot red pepper sauce*

*2 tablespoons (25 ml) Worcestershire sauce*

*2 tablespoons (25 ml) lemon juice*

*Salt and pepper to taste*

Preheat oven to 375°F (190°C). Place peppers and onion in
a bowl and toss lightly with olive oil. Spread on baking sheet
and roast until vegetables begin to brown (approximately
45 minutes). Allow to cool. Pulse artichokes a few times
in a blender until chunky and then add to cooled roasted
vegetables. Add salmon and cream cheese and mix together.
Add hot red pepper sauce, Worcestershire sauce, lemon juice,
salt, and pepper. Spoon into ceramic bowl or mold and bake
for about 1 hour, until top is golden brown. Serve warm with
crusty bread, toast points, or crackers.

**Executive Chef Scott Wells, Great Alaska Adventure Lodge,
Sterling, Alaska**

# Halibut Olympia

*serves two*

2 (6-ounce/170 g) skinless halibut fillets
2 to 4 ounces (55 to 115 g) fresh spinach
   (optional)
½ cup (129 g) mayonnaise
Salt and lemon pepper to taste
1 sprig fresh dill, chopped

Preheat oven to 350°F (180°C). Layer shallow roasting pan with spinach, if desired, and place fillets on top. Slather a ½- to ¾-inch (1.25 to 2 cm) layer of mayonnaise onto halibut, completely covering the top and all sides of the fillets. Season with salt, lemon pepper, and dill. Bake for 1 hour or until golden brown to slightly dark brown. Drain oil from pan and serve.

*Executive Chef Scott Wells, Great Alaska Adventure Lodge, Sterling, Alaska*

## Serving Size

- Plan to serve 6 to 8 ounces (170 to 226 g) of fish fillet per person for an entrée, or 10 to 12 ounces (280 to 340 g) of a whole fish.

# Smoked Salmon or Halibut Pâté

*serves eight to ten as an appetizer*

3 cups (700 ml) smoked salmon or
   halibut, broken into small pieces
1½ cups (355 ml) cream cheese, softened
   at room temperature and cut in
   large cubes
8 dashes hot red pepper sauce (add 4 extra
   dashes if using halibut)
2 tablespoons (30 ml) lemon juice
   (add 1 more tablespoon [15 ml]
   if using halibut)
2 tablespoons (6 g) dill
Salt and pepper to taste
Fresh dill, edible flowers, or lemon slices
   for garnish

Combine all ingredients in food processor and puree for approximately 3 minutes or until smooth. Put in mold or bowl lined with plastic wrap. Chill for at least 2 hours. Turn mold over and remove wrap. Smooth with knife and decorate as desired with dill, edible flowers, or lemon slices. Serve with toast points or crusty bread.

*Executive Chef Scott Wells, Great Alaska Adventure Lodge, Sterling, Alaska*

## Preparation Tips

■ *If you buy fish packaged in cellophane, don't buy a package that has liquid in it; it's a sure sign of being old.*
■ *Thaw fish slowly in the refrigerator to keep the texture in tact.*
■ *Don't ever put the flesh into water or in a microwave oven to thaw.*

# Catfish/Redfish Court-Bouillon

*serves four*

2 pounds (907 g) catfish or redfish fillets,
    skin removed, cut into large chunks
1½ teaspoons (9 g) salt
1 teaspoon (2 g) black pepper
1 teaspoon (2 g) red pepper flakes
1 yellow onion, finely chopped
1 cup (100 g) chopped green onions
⅓ cup (38 g) flour
½ cup (120 ml) cooking oil
1 (8-ounce/235 ml) can tomato sauce
1 cup (235 ml) water

Gently mix all ingredients in heavy pot and cover. Simmer over medium heat for 10 minutes. Shake pot to move ingredients. Do not stir or fish will break up. Cook another 10 minutes, until fish flakes when tested with a fork. Serve over hot cooked rice.

*Chef Gayle Fontenot, Grosse Savanne Waterfowl and Wildlife Lodge, Lake Charles, Louisiana*

GROSSE SAVANNE WATERFOWL AND WILDLIFE LODGE, Lake Charles, Louisiana

# Herb-Encrusted Fresh Reef Snapper with Tomatoes, Olives, Capers, and Herbs in a Cablia Buerre Blanc

*serves four*

2 cloves garlic

7 fresh basil leaves

¼ cup (20 g) grated Parmesan cheese

1 tablespoon (4 g) minced parsley

Pinch salt

Pinch pepper

1 cup (100 g) plain dry bread crumbs

4 (6-ounce/170 g) snapper fillets

1¼ cups (170 g) flour

3 eggs, whisked

4 tablespoons (60 ml) plus 2 tablespoons
    (30 ml) olive oil

1 small shallot, minced

1 clove garlic, minced

2 ripe tomatoes, chopped or
    1 12-ounce/340.2 g can tomatoes,
    drained and chopped

5 fresh basil leaves, minced

15 kalamata olives, pitted

1 teaspoon (2 g) capers

1 tablespoon (15 ml) Chardonnay

2 tablespoons (28 g) cold butter

Combine first 7 ingredients (garlic through bread crumbs) in food processor and chop for 30 seconds. Remove to a large bowl.

Preheat oven to 350°F (180°C). Dredge snapper fillets in flour to coat evenly. Place floured fish in whisked egg to coat evenly. Remove fillets from egg mixture one at a time and coat evenly with breadcrumb mixture.

Heat 4 tablespoons (60 ml) olive oil in skillet over medium heat until barely smoking. Place fillets in hot oil and brown lightly on each side, about 2 minutes per side. Transfer to baking sheet and finish in oven for 5 to 8 minutes, or until cooked through.

To hot skillet, add 2 tablespoons (30 ml) olive oil, shallot, garlic, tomatoes, basil, olives, and capers and sauté while stirring for 1 minute. Add wine and simmer for 30 seconds. Remove pan from heat, stir in cold butter, and pour sauce on fish.

***Hawk's Cay Resort and Marina, Duck Key, Florida***

HAWK'S CAY RESORT AND MARINA,
Duck Key, Florida

# Savory Seaside Grouper

*serves four*

2 cups (240 ml) lime juice

1 medium green bell pepper, seeded and
   finely chopped

1 clove garlic, minced

1 medium onion, finely chopped

¼ teaspoon (0.5 g) chopped and seeded
   chili pepper

¼ teaspoon (1.5 g) salt

Pinch of freshly ground black pepper

2 pounds (910 g) fresh grouper (or other
   mild white fish)

Oil for deep frying

¼ cup (32 g) all-purpose flour

2 eggs, beaten

1½ cups (160 g) fine dry bread crumbs

### Dipping Sauce

½ cup (120 ml) mayonnaise

2 tablespoons (30 ml) sweet pickle relish

½ teaspoon (3 ml) fresh grated or bottled
   horseradish

1 mango, peeled, pitted, and finely chopped

1 teaspoon (1.5 g) chopped fresh cilantro

1 tablespoon (15 ml) key lime juice

In a bowl, mix lime juice, bell pepper, garlic, onion, chili pepper, salt, and pepper to make marinade. Place marinade in a shallow dish and set aside 1 tablespoon (15 ml) of marinade to flavor the dipping sauce.

Wash and slice fish fillets into thin strips about 3 inches (7.5 cm) long, 1 inch (2.5 cm) wide, and ¼ inch (0.6 cm) thick. Place fish in dish with marinade, completely covering fillets, and marinate for 30 minutes.

In a large heavy pot, pour in oil to a depth of about 2 inches (5 cm). Heat oil to 325°F (170°C). Dip marinated fillets in flour, then eggs, and then bread crumbs. Deep-fry until golden brown.

To make Dipping Sauce, combine remaining ingredients (mayonnaise through lime juice) and reserved 1 tablespoon (15 ml) marinade. Serve Dipping Sauce with fish.

Excellent when served with salad or coleslaw.

*Hawk's Cay Resort and Marina, Duck Key, Florida*

# Potato Pancakes with Smoked Trout

*serves four as an appetizer*

2 medium russet potatoes

¼ cup (40 g) diced red onions

¼ cup (25 g) green onions

¼ teaspoon (0.5 g) ground nutmeg

1 egg

2 tablespoons (16 g) flour

Salt and pepper to taste

Canola oil for pan frying

4 small sprigs fresh dill

4 tablespoons (60 ml) sour cream

½ pound (226 g) smoked trout, broken
    into large, bite-sized chunks

Peel and quarter 1 potato and cook in boiling, salted water for 15 minutes or until tender. Drain and cool.

Peel the second potato, and grate into a bowl. Squeeze out excess water. Grate the cooked potato and combine with the grated raw potato. Add onions, nutmeg, egg, flour, salt, and pepper. Mix well.

Heat pan with oil and spoon batter into pan in heaping tablespoons. Flatten the potato mixture slightly in the pan. Brown both sides and let drain on paper towels. Garnish with dill, sour cream, and smoked trout, and serve.

*Henry's Fork Lodge, Island Park, Idaho*

HENRY'S FORK LODGE,
Island Park, Idaho

# Kids' Fish Sticks

*makes twenty finger-sized portions*

1 cup (125 g) flour
¼ cup (35 g) cornmeal
1 teaspoon (4.5 g) baking powder
1 teaspoon (1.5 g) Cajun seasoning
1 teaspoon (6 g) salt
½ teaspoon (1 g) black pepper
1 teaspoon (0.1 g) parsley flakes

½ cup (120 ml) buttermilk
1 egg, beaten

1½ cups (355 ml) half-and-half olive/
   canola oil blend
4 (6- to 8-ounce/170 to 225 g) fish fillets,
   cut into 1-ounce (28 g) strips

Combine flour, cornmeal, baking powder, Cajun seasoning, salt, pepper, and parsley flakes in one bowl, and buttermilk and egg in another. Dredge fish pieces in flour mixture, then buttermilk mixture, then again in flour mixture.

In a large skillet, heat oil to 325°F (170°C). Place pieces in heated oil; fry for approximately 6 to 8 minutes, turning every 2 minutes until golden brown. Serve with ketchup or tartar sauce.

*Highland Ranch, Philo, California*

HIGHLAND RANCH, *Philo, California*

# Slow-Roasted Largemouth Bass with Cucumber Salsa

*serves six to eight*

1 (6- to 8-pound/2.75 to 3.77 kg)
   largemouth bass, gutted and scaled (or
   2 or 3 smaller bass adding up to 6 to 8
   pounds/2.75 to 3.75 kg)
Salt and pepper
1 lemon, sliced in rounds
2 sprigs fresh dill
Olive oil
Kosher salt
Cucumber salsa

**Cucumber Salsa**
½ English cucumber, diced
½ plum tomato, diced
¼ red onion, diced
2 teaspoons (17 g) capers, rinsed and
   drained
1 lemon, juiced
Salt and pepper
1 sprig fresh dill, coarsely chopped

Preheat oven to 375°F (190°C). Season fish with salt and pepper. Place lemon slices and 2 sprigs of dill inside fish. Place fish on a baking sheet lined with parchment paper; coat fish with olive oil and sprinkle it lightly with salt.

Roast fish for 30 to 45 minutes, to an internal temperature of 125°F (52°C) when tested with an instant-read thermometer, or until the flesh flakes easily with a fork. If using smaller fish the cooking time will be shorter; check temperature and/or texture after 20 minutes.

Mix all salsa ingredients together and serve with fish.

**Highland Ranch, Philo, California**

# Baked Trout in Foil

*serves two*

---

2 fresh trout, gutted, scaled, heads and tails
   removed, and butterflied

Salt and freshly ground white pepper

Juice of ½ lemon

1½ tablespoons (20 g) Maître d'Hôtel
   butter (recipe follows), softened to room
   temperature

½ cup (125 g) unflavored white bread crumbs

Oil to coat foil

2 pieces of aluminum foil large enough to
   cover the fish, lightly oiled on 1 side

Lemon wedges for garnish

### Maître d'Hôtel Butter

*(makes ½ cup/120 ml)*

1 teaspoon (4.7 g) butter

1 teaspoon (2 g) finely chopped shallot

8 tablespoons (113 g) unsalted butter,
   softened at room temperature

1 tablespoon (15 ml) plus 1 teaspoon
   (5 ml) freshly squeezed lemon juice

½ teaspoon (1 g) finely chopped lemon zest

¼ teaspoon (1.5 g) salt

1 tablespoon (4 g) chopped fresh parsley

1 tablespoon (3 g) finely cut chives

½ teaspoon (7 ml) Worcestershire sauce

Season the inside of the trout lightly with salt, white pepper, and a squeeze of lemon juice, then spread with Maître d'Hôtel Butter. Sprinkle bread crumbs over the butter, fold trout halves together, and place on one half of the oiled foil. Fold foil loosely over trout and seal by crimping.

If you are not ready to grill or bake trout, refrigerate the trout package, up to 24 hours in advance, until ready to use. Refrigerated trout may take an extra minute to cook.

Preheat grill to high. Place foil-packaged trout on preheated grill for 2 to 3 minutes. Flip over on the grill and cook the other side for 2 to 3 minutes, then move to a cooler spot on the grill, such as the corners. Cook another 3 to 4 minutes. Do not overcook fish. Serve with lemon wedge.

For indoor cooking, preheat oven to 375°F (190°C). Place the trout package on preheated baking sheet and cook in oven for 6 to 7 minutes on each side.

Serve with small boiled potatoes with butter, salt, and freshly cut chives.

to make Maître d'Hôtel Butter, melt 1 teaspoon (4.7 g) butter in a saucepan over medium-low heat. Gently sauté shallot until soft, without browning. Transfer to a bowl and blend in remaining ingredients. Wrap well and refrigerate or freeze unused portion.

*Chef Rodger Martin, The Homestead, Hot Springs, Virginia*

The Homestead, Hot Springs, Virginia

# Sautéed Mountain Trout

*serves six*

½ cup (62 g) blanched, sliced almonds

½ cup (120 ml) half-and-half

Salt and freshly ground white pepper

1 cup (125 g) flour

2 fresh trout, gutted, scaled, heads and tails
  removed, and butterflied

Peanut oil for pan frying

6 tablespoons (85 g) butter

Juice of 3 lemons

1 tablespoon (4 g) chopped fresh parsley

½ cup (75 g) canned or peeled fresh grapes
  (4 to 5 per serving)

Sprigs of fresh parsley or dill

6 lemon wedges

Preheat oven to 250°F (120° C). Spread almonds on baking sheet and toast in oven until golden brown, about 15 minutes. Transfer to a bowl and reserve.

In another small bowl, mix half-and-half with some salt and pepper. Spread flour on wax paper or plate. Dip butterflied fillets carefully into half-and-half, coating both sides. Let excess drip off and then place fillets on the flour. Pat fillets lightly into flour, turn over, and repeat on other side. Remove and shake gently to remove excess flour. This step should be done just before you are ready to sauté fillets; otherwise they will be pasty.

Heat a frying pan over high heat. Fill with oil to a depth of ⅛ inch (3 mm). When oil is barely smoking, place trout in pan skin-side up. Do not crowd pan. Cook fillets in separate batches if necessary. Change the oil if it becomes clouded and smoky. When trout starts to sizzle, reduce heat to medium-high and cook for 3 minutes. Turn fillets over and after sizzling starts, sauté for 2 minutes. Remove to paper towels to drain, then place on warm serving platter or plate.

When all fillets are cooked, pour oil from pan and wipe out. Set pan back on stove over medium heat. Add butter to pan and swirl butter around as it melts, until it begins to turn light golden brown. When this happens, add lemon juice immediately to prevent butter from browning any further. Stir in parsley, almonds, and grapes; remove from heat, and pour sauce over fish. Garnish with sprigs of parsley or dill and lemon wedges. Serve at once.

*Chef Rodger Martin, The Homestead, Hot Springs, Virginia*

# Smoked Trout and Sunflower Seed Risotto

*serves four as an appetizer*

1 tablespoon (14 g) butter

2 (28 ml) tablespoons olive oil

1 small white onion, diced

Pinch salt

8 ounces (225 g) sunflower seed kernels

½ cup (120 ml) dry vermouth

4 cups (940 ml) water

Zest of 1 lemon

1 bunch green onions, sliced

3 tablespoons (45 ml) crème fraîche

1 (about 1 to 1¼ pounds/450 to 575 g)
     boneless smoked trout, roughly flaked

3 tablespoons (42 g) butter

¼ cup (20 g) grated Piave vecchio cheese
     (Parmesan, aged Gouda, or a combination
     of the two may be substituted in a pinch)

Freshly ground black pepper

Salt to taste

Melt butter and olive oil together in bottom of a pressure cooker. Add diced onion and sauté until tender. Season onions with a pinch of salt. Add sunflower seeds and continue to cook until seeds are lightly toasted. Add vermouth and scrape up any brown bits that may have formed. With lid off, cook until pan is nearly dry.

Add water and another pinch of salt. Cover the pressure cooker and cook under pressure for 45 minutes. When time is up, release the pressure, strain seeds, and reserve liquid separately. Purée one-third of the seeds in a blender with some of the cooking liquid until a smooth fluid puree is formed. Strain puree through a fine mesh sieve and mix with reserved sunflower seeds. This is the risotto base.

Heat risotto base in pot. Fold in lemon zest, green onions, crème fraîche, and flaked trout.  When hot, stir in butter to emulsify. Add half the cheese and season to taste with salt and pepper. Spoon risotto into bowls and top with remaining cheese and black pepper.

*Chef Alex Aki, Keyah Grande Resort, Pagosa Springs, Colorado*

KEYAH GRANDE, *Pagosa Springs, Colorado*

# Baked Stuffed Trout

*serves four*

---

**Stuffing:**

½ cup (80 g) chopped onions

½ cup (50 g) chopped celery

½ cup (60 g) chopped green pepper

½ cup (75 g) chopped red pepper

4 tablespoons (56 g) butter

1 cup (50 g) crumbled stale bread

1 tablespoon (7 g) Italian seasoning

1 teaspoon (3 g) garlic powder

A few drops hot red pepper sauce

4 whole trout, gutted and scaled

1 cup (140 g) cornmeal

1 cup (125 g) flour

*A funny story goes with this recipe—several years ago a fellow brought a 4-pound trout in and said he wanted to have it stuffed, and even though I didn't really have time to do it before dinner, I cleaned it, stuffed it, and presented it to him on a beautiful platter. Did his jaw drop, and my heart sink, when he said, "I meant I wanted a taxidermist to stuff it." He went back out to try to catch another fish to "stuff" but couldn't do it, and we haven't heard from him since!*

Preheat over to 350°F (180°C). In a sauté pan over medium-high heat, combine onions, celery, peppers, and butter and sauté until vegetables are tender. Combine vegetables, crumbled bread, Italian seasoning, garlic powder, and hot red pepper sauce. If the mixture is too dry, add more butter.

Clean fish thoroughly. Combine cornmeal and flour and coat trout thoroughly on all sides. Lay fish on greased baking sheet. Fill with stuffing and lay any extra stuffing around the fish. Cover with foil and bake for approximately 1 hour or until fish flakes easily with a fork.

*Libby Camps, Sporting Lodges and Outfitter, Ashland, Maine*

LIBBY CAMPS, SPORTING LODGES AND OUTFITTER, *Ashland, Maine*

# Poached Brook Trout

*serves one*

3 to 4 cups (700 to 950 ml) water
½ onion, sliced
2 lemon slices
1 bay leaf
Peppercorns
1 (10-inch/25 cm) brook trout

Heat water in a 12-inch (30 cm) nonstick frying pan. Add onion, lemon, bay leaf, and several peppercorns. Bring to just below a boil. Add brook trout and poach just a few minutes on each side.

**Libby Camps, Sporting Lodges and Outfitter, Ashland, Maine**

## How to Store Your Fish

■ *A good way to store fresh fish in the refrigerator is to wrap it tightly in plastic wrap or a reusable plastic bag and bury it in ice. Do this in the vegetable bin in your refrigerator or use a baking pan. Note: fish stays the freshest if it's between 32° and 35° (0° and 2°C).*

# Crunchy Flounder

*serves four*

1 cup (125 g) flour, seasoned with salt
   and pepper

4 eggs

¼ cup (15 g) chopped fresh parsley

1 teaspoon (1 g) chopped fresh dill

Zest of 2 lemons

Salt and pepper to taste

4 cups (435 g) panko (Japanese bread
   crumbs)

4 (6- to 8-ounce/170 to 225 g)
   flounder fillets

2 tablespoons (28 g) butter

2 tablespoons (28 ml) olive oil

Mix the seasoned flour in a large bowl. Crack eggs into
another bowl and whisk well. In a third bowl, combine
parsley, dill, lemon zest, salt, pepper, and panko.

Take the first fillet and dredge in the seasoned flour until
completely covered. Shake off excess flour. Dip fillet into the
whisked eggs, turning it over until completely covered. Then
move dipped fillet into the panko mixture, pressing it into
the surface so the panko mixture sticks well. Set aside. Repeat
with remaining fillets.

Heat butter and olive oil in a large skillet until barely
smoking. Place fillets into heated pan, skin-side up, and fry
on medium-high until deep golden brown. Flip fillets and fry
until second side is browned, about 3 to 4 minutes per side.
The fish is done when it flakes when poked with a fork.

*The Lodge on Little St. Simons Island, Little St. Simons
Island, Georgia*

THE LODGE ON
LITTLE ST. SIMON'S ISLAND, *Georgia*

# Grouper with Mango Salsa

*serves four*

4 (6 to 8-ounce/170 to 225 g)
   grouper fillets
1 tablespoon (15 ml) vegetable oil
Salt and white pepper
½ cup (120 ml) white wine (preferably
   Sauvignon Blanc)
4 ripe mangos, peeled and pitted
1 tablespoon (14 g) butter
1 tablespoon (15 ml) honey
Dash cayenne or habanero chili powder
2 tablespoons (28 g) butter
6 leaves fresh basil, chopped

Preheat grill on high. Coat grouper fillets with oil, then season with salt and white pepper. Grill 3 to 4 minutes per side or until the fillets develop dark brown grill marks and the flesh springs back readily when poked with a finger. Or, grill until internal temperature reaches 125°F (52°C) on instant-read thermometer inserted into the thickest part of the fish.

Meanwhile, reduce white wine over medium heat to ¼ cup (60 ml). Purée 2 of the mangos in the blender and dice the other two. In a separate skillet, sauté diced mangos with butter for 1 minute, turning once or twice. Add pureed mangos and wine and cook on low for 2 more minutes. Whisk in honey, cayenne pepper, butter, salt, and white pepper to taste.

To serve, top grouper with mango salsa and basil.

*The Lodge on Little St. Simons Island, Little St. Simons Island, Georgia*

# Stuffed Flounder

*serves four*

---

1 pound (455 g) jumbo lump crabmeat

½ red pepper, cored and diced

½ yellow pepper, cored and diced

¼ cup (15 g) chopped parsley

⅓ cup (80 ml) mayonnaise

2 tablespoons (28 ml) Worcestershire sauce

Splash hot red pepper sauce

Juice of one lemon

Salt and pepper to taste

4 tablespoons (55 g) butter

4 (6- to 8-ounce/170 to 225 g) flounder fillets

Paprika to taste

Lemon wedges to garnish

In medium bowl, mix crabmeat with peppers, parsley, mayonnaise, Worcestershire sauce, hot red pepper sauce, lemon juice, salt, and pepper.

Preheat broiler. Melt butter in a large skillet on medium-high heat. When foaming subsides, sauté fillets in butter, about 1 minute per side. Top with crabmeat mixture and sprinkle with paprika. Transfer to broiler and cook until light brown on top.

Serve immediately with lemon wedges.

***The Lodge on Little St. Simons Island, Little St. Simons Island, Georgia***

# Rainbow Trout with Poached Eggs

*serves four*

### Hollandaise Sauce

*1 egg yolk*

*1 cup (235 ml) clarified butter (available
    in supermarkets as ghee)*

*Pinch of cayenne pepper*

*Juice of ½ lime*

*Salt to taste*

### Fish

*4 whole boneless trout, heads and tails on*

*4 tablespoons (60 ml) olive oil*

*Salt and pepper to taste*

*2 tablespoons (30 ml) white vinegar*

*4 eggs*

*4 slices brioche toasts, cut into triangles*

In a medium-sized stainless steel bowl, whisk egg yolk while gently heating over a lit burner. When the yolk lightens in color, remove from heat and very slowly add 1 tablespoon (14 g) of clarified butter while whisking constantly. When butter is fully incorporated, add another tablespoon (14 g) and continue whisking until incorporated. Repeat until all the butter is incorporated into the egg yolk and the mixture has thickened considerably. Whisk in the cayenne pepper, lime juice, and salt. Cover hollandaise sauce and keep warm but not hot.

Preheat broiler to high. Rub trout with olive oil and sprinkle with salt and pepper. Broil for 3 minutes or until the flesh flakes easily when poked with a fork.

Add vinegar to 1 quart (1 liter) water in a shallow pan. Bring to a simmer (not a boil) and gently drop eggs into simmering water for 3 minutes. Remove with a slotted spoon and drain on paper towels.

To serve, place the broiled trout on individual dinner plates. Top each trout with a poached egg and some Hollandaise Sauce. Serve with brioche toasts.

***The Lodge on Little St. Simons Island, Little St. Simons Island, Georgia***

# Maple Drunken Salmon Rosettes

*serves four*

4 (6- to 8-ounce/170 to 225 g)
    salmon fillets

**Marinade**

¼ cup (60 ml) maple sugar or pure
    maple syrup

¼ cup (60 ml) whiskey

3 tablespoons (25 g) minced garlic

¼ cup (60 ml) soy sauce

2 quick pours of ketjap manis (available
    from Asian grocers)

2 tablespoons (28 ml) olive oil

2 tablespoons (12 g) orange zest

Slice salmon on an angle to form petal-shaped slices. Layer slices so that they overlap slightly and roll up into a rose. Combine remaining ingredients and cover salmon. Marinate for approximately 6 hours.

After salmon has marinated, preheat oven to 400°F (200°C). Remove salmon from marinade and bake for 20 to 25 minutes or until the salmon is cooked through.

*Chef Heather Davis, Nimmo Bay Resort, Port McNeill, British Columbia*

NIMMO BAY RESORT
Port McNeill, British Colombia

# Crispy Fish with Lemon-Caper Sauce

*serves four*

2 pounds (910 g) skinless fish fillets (pike, pickerel, or other firm white fish)

2 tablespoons (28 ml) dry white vermouth

1 bay leaf

6 tablespoons (90 ml) olive oil

½ cup (63 g) flour

½ teaspoon (3 g) salt

½ teaspoon (0.4 g) Dymond Lake Seasoning (recipe follows) or ¼ teaspoon (0.5 g) black pepper

2 eggs, lightly beaten

1½ cups (165 g) dry bread crumbs

Oil for frying

**Dymond Lake Seasoning**

1 teaspoon (2 g) seasoned pepper

½ teaspoon (3 g) salt

¼ teaspoon (0.5 g) oregano

1 teaspoon (0.15 g) celery flakes

1 tablespoon (0.35 g) parsley flakes

**Lemon Caper Sauce:**

6 tablespoons (85 g) butter or margarine

1 garlic clove, crushed

2 teaspoons (2.5 g) chopped fresh parsley or ½ teaspoon (0.1 g) dried

1 teaspoon (1.3 g) chopped fresh oregano or ⅓ teaspoon (0.6 g) dried

2 tablespoons (17 g) chopped capers

2 tablespoons (28 ml) lemon juice

Lemon and parsley (for garnish)

Place fillets in a large, shallow nonmetal dish. In a small saucepan, combine vermouth, bay leaf, and oil and heat gently. Allow to cool completely and then pour over fillets. Marinate for 1 hour, turning occasionally.

Preheat oven to 150°F (75°C). Mix flour with salt and Dymond Lake Seasoning or pepper. Remove fish from marinade and dredge with flour. Dip fillets into egg, then coat with bread crumbs. In a large frying pan, heat ¼ inch (8 mm) of oil (no more) until barely smoking. Add fillets and cook over medium heat until golden, approximately 3 minutes per side. Remove and drain on a wire rack. Keep warm in a 150°F (75°C) oven.

To make Lemon Caper Sauce, pour oil out of pan and wipe clean. Add butter and garlic and cook on medium until lightly browned. Add parsley, oregano, capers, and lemon juice.

To serve: Arrange fillets on serving tray or individual plates and pour sauce on top. Garnish with lemon and parsley.

*North Knife Lake Lodge, Thompson, Manitoba*

NORTH KNIFE LAKE LODGE
Thompson, Manitoba

# Fish Balls with Honey-Dill Sauce

*makes about thirty*

---

### Honey-Dill Sauce:

1½ cups (360 g) mayonnaise

1 cup (235 ml) honey

2 teaspoons (2 g) dried dill

### Fish Balls

Vegetable oil for deep-frying

1 cup (155 g) flaked cooked fish

1 cup (210 g) mashed potatoes

2 eggs

1 cup (115 g) fine cracker crumbs, divided

2 tablespoons (7 g) Dymond Lake
    Seasoning or black pepper

1 teaspoon (1 g) dried dill

¼ cup (25 g) Parmesan cheese

### Dymond Lake Seasoning:

2 teaspoons (4 g) pepper

1 teaspoon (7 g) salt

½ teaspoon (1 g) oregano

2 teaspoons (0.3 g) celery flakes

2 tablespoons (0.8 g) parsley flakes

*"How many fish have you caught, mister?" asked a boy, seeing an old man fishing on the banks of a stream. "Well, son," answered the aged angler thoughtfully, "if I catch this one I'm after, and two more, then I'll have three."*

To make Honey-Dill Sauce, combine mayonnaise, honey, and dill. Store in refrigerator until ready to serve.

Heat oil in a deep fryer or heavy pot to 375°F (190°C). (Oil in heavy pot should be about 3 inches (7.5 cm) deep; follow manufacturer's recommendation for deep fryer.) Combine fish, potatoes, eggs, ½ cup (58 g) cracker crumbs, Dymond Lake Seasoning, dill, and cheese, and mix well. Form into 1-inch (2.5 cm) balls and roll in remaining cracker crumbs to coat fish balls. Drop fish balls carefully into oil and fry until a deep golden brown, about 3 to 4 minutes. Drain and serve with Honey-Dill Sauce.

**North Knife Lake Lodge, Thompson, Manitoba**

# Mustard-Dill Sauce

*makes 1¼ cups (295 ml)*

1 cup (235 ml) mayonnaise or
  salad dressing
¼ cup (60 ml) prepared mustard
1 teaspoon (1 g) dried dill

Combine all ingredients and serve over trout, salmon, or other game fish.  Store leftover sauce in refrigerator for up to a month.

*North Knife Lake Lodge, Thompson, Manitoba*

## Deep-Frying Tips

■ *If you're going to deep-fry, the pan you choose to use is very important. Choose a heavy pot so if you nudge it, the pot filled with hot oil won't budge!*

■ *Think about what you have to fry, and choose the depth and diameter that will work to float numerous fish pieces with air between them when the pot is half-full of oil.*

■ *You can also use a wok or electric deep fryer that has a built-in thermometer that keeps oil at a constant temperature. Use what works for your cooking style.*

■ *Consider investing in a frying basket or a spider for small amounts of fish. A spider looks like a metal web and has a long handle and can lower and raise fish from the hot oil.*

■ *Also consider investing in a deep-fry thermometer, which will help you gauge oil temperature as you cook.*

■ *Choose corn, peanut, and safflower oil for frying because they can get really hot without burning. If you experiment, you can find the oil with the flavor that you enjoy most. Try olive oil, too. It can't go to the high heat of peanut oil, but the taste is unique and you may enjoy it.*

# Local Grouper, Shellfish, Okra, and Bouillabaisse Broth

*serves six*

### Bouillabaisse

*1 tablespoon (15 ml) vegetable oil*

*1 medium onion, peeled and roughly chopped*

*2 carrots, peeled and roughly chopped*

*4 celery stalks, roughly chopped*

*5 cloves garlic, minced*

*½ cup (130 g) tomato paste*

*Pinch saffron*

*1 cup (235 ml) white wine*

*2 pounds (900 g) fish bones, mussels, shrimp shells, and lobster bodies*

### Pilaf

*6 to 8 strips of bacon, chopped*

*1 small onion, chopped*

*4 cups (940 ml) bouillabaisse broth*

*2 cups (370 g) long-grain rice*

*1 tomato, blanched, skinned, and chopped*

*6 (5-ounce/142 g) pieces grouper*

*Salt and pepper to taste*

*1½ cups (355 ml) bouillabaisse broth*

*1 sprig fresh tarragon*

*Juice of ⅛ lemon*

Heat the vegetable oil in a large (12-inch/30 cm) frying pan set over medium-low heat. Add onion, carrots, celery, and garlic, and cook gently without browning for 10 minutes, stirring occasionally. Add tomato paste and cook while stirring occasionally for 10 minutes.

In a separate saucepan, add saffron to white wine and heat to a simmer. Add to vegetables. Add fish bones, mussels, shrimp shells, and lobster bodies. Cover with water and simmer for 1 hour. Strain through cheesecloth and reserve broth. Cool.

For Pilaf, heat saucepan set over medium heat. Add bacon and cook until crispy. Add onion and cook until translucent, then add bouillabaisse broth and bring to a boil. Add rice, stirring until it boils. Boil 1½ minutes and keep stirring to ensure rice does not stick. Turn off heat, stir for 30 seconds, and cover for 6 minutes. Add chopped tomato and stir until tomato is evenly distributed, then cover for 5 more minutes.

Preheat oven to 425°F (220°C). Remove fish from refrigerator and bring it to room temperature. Season with salt and pepper.

Put bouillabaisse broth into a deep pot. Add sprig of tarragon, squeeze lemon into pot, and add a pinch of salt. Heat but do not boil.

*continued on next page*

THE INN AT PALMETTO BLUFF,
Bluffton, South Carolina

# Local Grouper, Shellfish, Okra, and Bouillabaisse Broth

*continued*

3 tablespoons (84 g) clarified
    butter, divided (available at most
    supermarkets as ghee)
1 link of andouille sausage, roughly
    chopped
6 to 10 okra, sliced
12 mussels
12 clams
1 cup (235 ml) chicken stock
6 medium shrimp, peeled, deveined,
    and coarsely chopped
1 teaspoon (0.8 g) dried thyme
3½ tablespoons (98 g) butter
Green onions for garnish

Have 3 medium-sized, oven-safe hot pans ready (2 for fish and 1 for rice). Add 1 tablespoon (14 g) clarified butter to each of the first 2 pans. When butter nears smoking point, add fish and cook until both sides are golden brown. Put pans into oven for 3 to 6 minutes.

In third pan, add remaining tablespoon (28 g) clarified butter. When butter melts, add sausage and okra and cook until slightly browned. Drain fat. Add ¼ cup (60 ml) of bouillabaisse, then add chicken stock, clams, and mussels. Add rice. Simmer for 3 minutes, then add shrimp and salt and pepper to taste. Keep warm until fish is ready. Remove fish from oven; add thyme and 1 tablespoon (14 g) butter to each pan and briefly baste. Remove fish from pan. Place seared-side up on paper towel. To finish rice, add remaining butter and stir until creamy.

To serve, place rice with mussels and clams on serving platter and top with fish. Serve hot.

**The Inn at Palmetto Bluff, Blufton, South Carolina**

# Cast-Iron Charred Salmon with Edamame, Jicama-Savoy Cabbage Slaw, and Pineapple Glaze

*serves four*

3 cups (465 g) pineapple

½ cup (235 ml) water, divided

¼ cup (60 ml) plus 3 tablespoons (45 ml) soy sauce

1½ cups (150 g) shelled and parboiled edamame (available from Asian grocers)

2 teaspoons (20 g) minced shallot

½ teaspoon (3 g) butter

Salt and freshly ground pepper to taste

1½ pounds (682 g) fresh salmon fillet, cut into 4 equal portions

1 carrot, cut into small matchsticks

½ English cucumber, cut into small matchsticks

1 cup (150 g) jicama, cut into small matchsticks

2 red jalapeños, ribs and seeds removed, cut into small matchsticks

1 cup (90 g) savoy cabbage, cut into small matchsticks

½-inch (1.25 cm) piece of ginger, peeled and cut into a small matchsticks

5 scallions, washed and finely cut diagonally

2 tablespoons (30 g) fresh wasabi paste

3 tablespoons (45 ml) light olive oil

Heat a cast-iron frying pan over high heat while preparing the rest of the meal. (Even a commercial stove cannot overheat the skillet for this dish, so don't be afraid to let it get really hot. Don't attempt this without good ventilation.)

In a heavy-bottomed stainless steel pot, cook the pineapple with ¼ cup (60 ml) water over medium heat until very tender. Allow the pineapple to cool for 10 minutes, then puree in a blender with the ¼ cup (60 ml) soy sauce until very smooth and thick. Chill in the refrigerator until ready to serve.

In a small pot, gently heat the edamame with the shallot, butter, remaining water, salt, and pepper. You want the beans to be hot but still a vibrant green (not overcooked to a drab olive green).

Season the salmon with salt and pepper on all sides and set aside. Combine all of the matchstick vegetables and the scallions in a bowl. In a separate bowl, mix together the wasabi paste and the 3 tablespoons (45 ml) soy sauce to make a thick dressing. Toss the vegetables with the soy-wasabi dressing.

Drizzle the olive oil over the salmon and sear for 20 to 25 seconds per side for rare salmon. If you prefer your salmon cooked more, allow it to continue cooking, turning in the pan frequently, for up to 10 minutes per inch (2.5 cm) of thickness for a well-done piece of fish.

To serve, place a spoonful of the pineapple glaze on a plate and a spoonful of the edamame next to it. Slice the salmon and lay over the edamame. Arrange the salad between the pineapple glaze and the tuna.

*Tom Donohoe, Executive Chef, Rainbow Ranch, Big Sky, Montana*

RAINBOW RANCH, *Big Sky, Montana*

# Pan-Seared Flathead Lake Whitefish with Warm Fingerling Potato Salad

*serves six*

## Whitefish

*1 teaspoon (2 g) ground fennel*
*1 teaspoon (1.8 g) ground coriander*
*1 teaspoon (3.3 g) ground mustard seed*
*2 tablespoons (36 g) kosher salt*
*6 whitefish fillets*

## Potato Salad

*½ pound (225 g) Russian banana*
*    fingerling potatoes (or other small*
*    potatoes), cut into ¼-inch (1 cm) discs*
*2 cloves garlic, chopped*
*1 large leek, white part only, cut into*
*    ¼-inch (1 cm) dice*
*1 tablespoon (15 ml) canola oil*
*2 medium apples, chopped and placed in*
*    water with a squeeze of lemon juice*
*3 tablespoons (45 ml) extra-virgin olive oil*
*2 teaspoons (10 ml) red wine vinegar*
*1 tablespoon (16 g) stone-ground mustard*

*Zest of 1 lemon (reserve juice)*
*Salt and pepper*
*2 tablespoons (28 g) cold salted butter*

Preheat oven to 350°F (180°C). Combine fennel, coriander, mustard seed, and kosher salt in a bowl. Season each fillet generously with seasoning mixture. Heat a cast-iron skillet with canola oil until barely smoking. Place fillets in hot pan, flesh-side down, and sear until golden brown, about 3 to 4 minutes. Flip fillets over in pan and place in oven for about 5 minutes or until fillets flake easily when poked with a fork. Keep warm until ready to serve.

Place potato discs in a pot with salted cold water and bring to a simmer. Cook just until tender, about 7 to 10 minutes. Drain potatoes and spread out on a tray to cool. Sauté garlic and leek in canola oil until tender and turn off heat. When pan cools to the touch, add apples and cooled potatoes and combine gently.

Whisk together olive oil, red wine vinegar, and mustard in a small bowl, then pour over potato, leek, and apple mixture. Toss in lemon zest, salt, and pepper.

In a small saucepan, heat lemon juice and reduce by half. Remove from heat; add butter and let it melt. Place fillets and potato salad on a serving plate. Pour lemon juice and butter mixture over fish and potato salad and serve.

Wine pairing:  Pike and Joyce Sauvignon Blanc, Australia

*Chef Jacob Wetherington, The Resort at Paws Up, Greenough, Montana*

THE RESORT AT PAWS UP, Greenough, Montana

# Salmon Wrapped in Rice Paper

*serves two as an appetizer*

2 sheets rice paper (available from Asian
   grocers)
1 ounce (28 ml) hoisin sauce (in the Asian
   section of most supermarkets)
1 ripe avocado
4 ounces (115 g) cooked salmon

Soak the rice paper sheets in warm water until soft and
pliable. Remove and drain on paper towels. Spread half the
hoisin sauce down the center of each rice paper sheet, leaving
1 inch (2.5 cm) on each end. Peel avocado and cut into
¼-inch (0.6 cm) slices. Lay slices on top of hoisin sauce.
Crumble half the salmon across the avocado on each sheet.
Roll rice paper around filling, tucking edges in as you go.
Slice each roll once on the bias and serve.

*Chef Gerard Thompson, Rough Creek Lodge and Resort,
Glen Rose, Texas*

ROUGH CREEK LODGE AND RESORT,
Glen Rose, Texas

# Rainbow Trout and Cucumber Nori Roll with Chili Garlic Sauce

*serves six*

1½ cups (280 g) jasmine rice
3 cups (705 ml) water
1 teaspoon (6 g) kosher salt
2 large portobello mushrooms
2 ounces (60 ml) grape seed oil
6 fillets rainbow trout
Kosher salt
Fresh coarsely ground black pepper
¼ cup (60 ml) hoisin sauce
1 red bell pepper
1 cucumber
6 sheets nori paper

### Chili Garlic Sauce

1 small shallot, minced
¼ cup (60 ml) chili garlic sauce
   (available at most Asian markets)
½ teaspoon (1 g) freshly ground
   black pepper
¼ cup (60 ml) soy sauce
¼ cup rice wine vinegar
½ tablespoon (1.5 g) chopped chives or
   cilantro
1 cup (240 g) mango puree
Kosher salt to taste

### Rice

Combine rice, water, and salt in a medium sauce-pan. Bring to a boil, stir briefly, reduce heat and simmer covered for 20 minutes or until rice is tender and water has been absorbed. Remove from heat and let stand covered until ready to assemble the rolls. If using a rice cooker, follow manufacturer's cooking instructions.

### Nori Rolls

Preheat oven to 350°F (180°C). Cut portobello mushrooms into ½-inch (1.25 cm) strips. Brush baking sheet with grape seed oil. Place trout fillets and portobello mushroom strips on cookie sheet. Season with salt and pepper. Brush the trout fillets with hoisin sauce. Bake in oven for 10 to 12 minutes or until trout is cooked through. Remove from oven and cover loosely with foil to keep warm until ready to serve.

Cut red bell pepper and cucumber into ¼-inch (0.6 cm) strips. Lay one sheet of nori paper on a cutting board or clean flat work surface. Spread 1 cup warm steamed rice on half of the nori paper. Place 1 trout fillet and 2 strips each of portobello mushroom, cucumber, and red pepper along the width of the rice. Moisten the end of the nori paper with warm water and roll it into a log shape, using the moistened end to seal the log closed. Repeat with remaining ingredients. Slice each log into 5 or 6 slices and serve with Chili Garlic Sauce.

To make Chili Garlic Sauce, combine all ingredients and mix well.

*Chef Gerard Thompson, Rough Creek Lodge and Resort, Glen Rose, Texas*

# Catfish and Tropical Fruit Ceviche

*serves two*

1 pound (455 g) fresh catfish fillet
Kosher salt and cracked black pepper
1 cup (235 ml) dry white wine
½ cup (60 g) diced mango
½ cup diced (60 g) papaya
½ cup diced (100 g) tomato
½ cup (110 g) diced avocado
¼ cup (40 g) diced grilled red onion
1 jalapeño, roasted and chopped
¼ cup (60 ml) fresh lime juice
2 tablespoons (28 ml) olive oil
2 tablespoons (8 g) chopped cilantro
2 tablespoons (8 g) chopped mint

Preheat oven to 375°F (190°C). Cut catfish into small bite-sized pieces. Spread on rimmed baking sheet and season with salt and pepper. Pour wine over fish and bake 7 minutes. Remove from oven, cool and set aside. Fold fish and remaining ingredients together. Season with salt and pepper.

*Chef Gerard Thompson, Rough Creek Lodge and Resort, Glen Rose, Texas*

## Wine Pairing Tip

*If you're creating a dish with intense flavor, choose an accompanying wine with intense flavor as well.*

*This can take a little experimentation. You can complement the food, or you can contrast the flavors and textures of the food with the wine—playing off tannin against fat, fruit against spice, complex against simple. The right combination will bring out the best in both the wine and the food, with neither one overpowering the other.*

*For example, food that is poached, steamed, sautéed, stir-fried, pan-fried, braised, roasted, broiled, grilled, or blackened might be respectively matched to wines based on (in rough order of intensity):*

### White Wines
- Chenin Blanc
- Riesling
- Sauvignon Blanc
- Chardonnay

### Red Wines
- Pinot noir
- Merlot
- Zinfandel
- Cabernet sauvignon
- Syrah

# Pan-Fried Trout

*serves four*

---

*2 medium eggs, beaten*

*1 cup (125 g) flour*

*1 cup (140 g) cornmeal*

*1 teaspoon (3 g) granulated garlic powder*

*½ teaspoon (3 g) salt*

*½ teaspoon (1 g) freshly ground
     black pepper*

*4 fresh trout fillets, skin and pin bones
     removed*

*1 lemon*

Set up two dredging stations using shallow bowls or containers. Put the beaten eggs in the first. In the second, combine flour, cornmeal, garlic powder, salt, and pepper. Thoroughly dredge each piece of trout in egg, then coat both sides completely with flour mixture.

Spray a large nonstick skillet with olive oil to thinly coat the bottom. Heat pan on medium-high. Fry fillets in preheated skillet until golden brown on both sides.

To serve, squeeze half of the lemon over cooked fish and cut the other half into 4 wedges to garnish each plate.

***Chef Caitlyn Luyten, Siwash Lake Ranch, 70 Mile House, British Columbia***

Siwash Lake Ranch, 70 Mile House, British Columbia

# Porcini-Dusted Steelhead, "Florentine" Orzo, Tomato Confit, and Balsamic Brown Butter Emulsion

*serves two*

2 plum tomatoes, halved lengthwise, seeds
   scooped out

2 sprigs fresh thyme

Olive oil as needed

6 ounces (170 g) spinach, cleaned and
   heavy stems removed

1 tablespoon (8 g) porcini dust (available
   from gourmet retailers)

¼ cup (30 g) flour

2 skinless steelhead fillets

Salt and pepper

1 tablespoon (15 ml) olive oil

¼ teaspoon (0.75 g) minced garlic

¼ cup (60 ml) white wine (preferably
   Chardonnay)

½ cup (120 ml) heavy cream

1½ cups (240 g) cooked orzo pasta,
   prepared according to directions

Ground white pepper

3 tablespoons (42 g) unsalted butter

1½ tablespoons (22 ml) balsamic
   vinegar

### Tomato confit

Preheat oven to 325°F (170°C). Place tomatoes and thyme in small sauté pan and cover with olive oil. Cover and bake for 20 minutes. When cool, remove skins from tomatoes and chop roughly.

### Spinach

Blanch spinach in salted boiling water for three seconds and plunge into ice water. Squeeze spinach dry, chop, and reserve.

### Steelhead

Preheat oven to 350°F (180°C). In mixing bowl, whisk porcini dust and flour together. Season filets with salt and pepper, then dredge in porcini dust mixture. Heat 1 tablespoon (15 ml) oil in 12-inch (30 cm) frying pan over medium-high heat until barely smoking. Fry filets until lightly browned. Flip fillets over in pan and place in oven for 5 minutes or until flesh flakes easily.

In 6-inch (15 cm) sauté pan, gently cook garlic over medium heat in small amount of oil. Add wine and reduce to about 1 tablespoon (15 ml). Add cream. Reduce cream by one-third and add chopped spinach and orzo pasta. Gently heat and season to taste with salt and ground white pepper.

Slowly cook butter in small frying pan until slightly brown. Pour balsamic vinegar into small mixing bowl. Slowly whisk in browned butter. Season with salt and pepper.

To serve, spoon spinach mixture onto each plate. Place steelhead on top of spinach mixture. Place tomato confit on top of steelhead. Drizzle balsamic brown butter emulsion around plate.

*Chef Kevin Humphreys, Snake River Lodge and Spa, Teton Village, Wyoming*

SNAKE RIVER LODGE AND SPA,
Teton Village, Wyoming

# Salmon with Chipotle-Lime Beurre Blanc

*serves four*

### Salmon

*4 (6- to 8-ounce/170 to 225 g) salmon
    fillets, skin on*
*Salt to taste*
*Finely ground peppercorn mixture or
    black pepper*
*1 tablespoon (15 ml) olive or canola oil*

### Chipotle-Lime Buerre Blanc

*¼ cup (40 g) finely chopped white onion*
*3 tablespoons (45 ml) puree of chipotle
    peppers in adobo sauce (available in the
    Mexican section of most supermarkets)*
*1 pound (455 g) butter, cut into ½-inch
    (1.25 cm) cubes, plus 1 tablespoon
    (14 g)*
*Juice of 4 limes*
*½ bottle (750 ml) white wine*
*Zest of 4 limes (reserve a little for garnish)*
*¼ cup (4 g) chopped fresh cilantro (reserve
    a little for garnish)*
*2 tablespoons (28 ml) heavy cream*

Preheat oven to 400°F (200°C). Season flesh side of each fillet with salt and pepper. Heat the oil in a large frying pan on medium-high heat until barely smoking. Place flesh side of fish down in hot pan and cook until a golden-brown crust forms. Turn fish over onto a baking sheet lined with parchment paper. When all fish is seared, place in oven for 5 to 8 minutes and bake just until firm.

To make the buerre blanc, combine onion, chipotle puree, and 1 tablespoon (14 g) butter in a 12-inch (30 cm) frying pan. Cook over medium-high heat, until onion is transparent but not brown. Add lime juice and wine and cook until most of the liquid has evaporated, then reduce heat to medium. While continuously whisking, add cubed butter, a little at a time, until well blended. Finish sauce with lime zest, chopped cilantro, and heavy cream while whisking the mixture.

To serve, drizzle some sauce onto fish and garnish with lime zest and cilantro. Serve remaining sauce on the side.

***Chef Aaron Stump, Spotted Horse Ranch, Jackson Hole, Wyoming***

**SPOTTED HORSE RANCH, Jackson Hole, Wyoming**

# Pesto-Crusted Trout

*serves four*

1 loaf stale French bread

1 (2-ounces/60 ml) jar basil pesto

¼ cup (40 g) shredded Parmesan cheese

¼ cup (25 g) flour

1 teaspoon (15 ml) salt

1 teaspoon (15 ml) coarsely ground
    peppercorn mix

¼ teaspoon (2 g) cayenne pepper

3 eggs

4 whole trout, gutted, scaled, deboned, and
    butterflied

2 tablespoons (30 ml) vegetable oil

Combine French bread, pesto, and parmesan cheese in food processor and pulse until combined but still a little chunky. Combine flour, salt, peppercorn mix, and cayenne pepper in a shallow pan and mix well. Crack eggs into a shallow pan and whisk. Dredge just the flesh side of the trout in the flour, then in the egg, and then in the pesto mix. Repeat until all trout are coated.

Heat oil in a large (12-inch/30 cm) nonstick frying pan on high. Place trout in a hot skillet, breaded-side down and cook until a golden brown crust has formed, approximately 5 minutes. Flip and cook other side for approximately 3 minutes or until it is cooked through but not dry.

**Chef Aaron Stump, Spotted Horse Ranch, Jackson Hole, Wyoming**

# Grilled Perch with Rhubarb Chutney Relish

*serves four*

### Chutney

1 cup (235 ml) honey
1 cup (235 ml) vinegar, balsamic
    or red wine
1 bunch fresh mint or peppermint
1 tablespoon (10 g) minced fresh ginger
1 tablespoon (15 g) mustard or mustard
    seed (optional)
2 cups (244 g) rhubarb, cleaned
    and chopped

### Perch

8 skinless perch fillets
1 tablespoon (15 ml) salad oil
Salt and pepper to taste

In a 2- to 4-quart (1.8 to 3.7 liter) saucepan, lightly brown honey by heating it for 4 to 5 minutes over medium heat while gently stirring. Add vinegar, mint, ginger, and mustard (if desired). Mix rhubarb chunks into mixture and cook over low heat for 10 to 12 minutes, until rhubarb begins to break down. Keep warm until ready to serve.

Preheat grill to high. Preheat oven to 375°F (190°C).

Brush fillets with oil and season with salt and pepper. Sear on hot grill for 2 minutes on each side. Transfer to baking sheet and put in oven to finish cooking for 3 to 5 minutes.

To serve, place two fillets on each dinner plate. Top with rhubarb chutney and serve immediately.

*Chef John Noel Gilbertson, CEC, Spring Lake Hunting Lodge and Resort, Oldham, South Dakota*

SPRING LAKE HUNTING LODGE
AND RESORT, Oldham, South Dakota

# Smoked Trout Crostini with Fennel-Cumin Yogurt

*serves six to eight as an appetizer*

1 teaspoon (3.5 g) mustard seeds

1 teaspoon (1.8 g) coriander seeds

1 teaspoon (2 g) fennel seeds

2 tablespoons (26 g) granulated sugar

Kosher salt

2 whole trout, gutted, scaled, boned, and
head and fins removed

Wood chips for smoking

1 bulb fennel, fronds saved

Extra-virgin olive oil

½ teaspoon (1 g) cumin seeds

½ cup (115 g) yogurt

1 good-quality French baguette

Freshly ground pepper

In small frying pan, toast mustard, coriander, and fennel seeds together until fragrant. Transfer to bowl and add sugar and 2 tablespoons (36.5 g) kosher salt.

Place trout in casserole dish and spread spice mixture over it. Cover with plastic and refrigerate for 6 hours. Rinse lightly to remove spices. Soak wood chips in water for 15 minutes. Using stovetop or standing smoker, prepare fire for smoking according to manufacturer's directions. Remove wood chips from water and place over fire in metal pan. Place trout in smoker. Check periodically to ensure it is smoking properly. Once smoke subsides, remove trout and let cool.

Preheat oven to 350°F (180°C). Remove core from fennel and dice small. In sauté pan, add enough olive oil to cover the bottom. Sauté fennel for 3 to 4 minutes or until soft. Pull from heat and let cool.

In small sauté pan, toast cumin seeds until fragrant. Transfer to bowl and cover with yogurt. Add cooled fennel to yogurt mix and season to taste. Slice baguette on the bias to make long crostini. Place on baking sheet, drizzle with olive oil, and season with salt and pepper. Place in oven and toast until golden brown. Remove and let cool. Once trout is cooled, remove skin and break up into pieces. Place on crostini, spoon yogurt over the top, and garnish with reserved fennel fronds.

*Chef Colton Soelberg, Sundance Resort, Sundance, Utah*

SUNDANCE RESORT, Sundance, Utah

# Pancetta-Wrapped Trout with Griddled Polenta, Roasted Root Vegetables, and Sherry Pan Vinaigrette

*serves four*

### Polenta

*Olive oil as needed*
*½ yellow onion, cut into small dice*
*2 cloves garlic, slivered*
*3 cups (700 ml) water*
*1 cup (275 g) polenta (medium-ground cornmeal)*
*Salt and pepper*
*1 cup (110 g) grated Gruyère or Gouda cheese*

### Roasted Root Vegetables

*1 large golden beet*
*Olive oil*
*Kosher salt*
*Freshly ground pepper*
*½ pint (115 g) pearl onions*
*1 medium carrot, peeled and diced*
*¼ turnip, peeled and diced*
*2 parsnips, peeled and diced*
*A few pats butter*

In large stainless steel pot, add enough oil to barely cover bottom and turn to medium-low heat. Add onion and garlic and cook gently over medium heat for 5 minutes, stirring occasionally.

Add water and bring to a boil. Add one third of the polenta and whisk until mixture resumes boiling. Add the second third of the polenta and stir while cooking for a few minutes. Add the final third of the polenta and stir until it resumes boiling. Reduce heat to low and cook, stirring occasionally (taking care that it doesn't stick to the pan bottom and burn), for 1 to 1½ hours. Season to taste with salt and pepper. Add cheese and cook 2 minutes longer. Pour into ovenproof 9 x 13-inch (22.5 x 32.5 cm) dish. Cool in refrigerator for at least 1 hour or until firm. Cut into 4 squares, triangles, circles, or other preferred shape. Set aside in refrigerator.

Preheat oven to 375°F (190°C). Put beet in ovenproof dish large enough to hold it with some room around it. Rub with olive oil, salt, and pepper. Add just enough water to barely cover the bottom of dish. Cover dish with foil and roast in oven for 1½ hours or until beet is easily pierced with a knife. Remove and let cool.

To loosen the skins of the pearl onions, bring 3 quarts (3 liters) water to a boil with a pinch of salt. Drop pearl onions in for 30 to 40 seconds, then strain and let cool.

Toss carros and turnip in olive oil, season with salt and pepper, and roast until slightly browned around the edges and soft to the bite (usually 45 minutes). Toss parsnips in olive oil, season with salt and pepper, and place in ovenproof dish. Cover with foil for first 20 minutes of cooking, then remove foil and allow to caramelize.

*continued on next page*

### Pancetta-Wrapped Trout

*4 tablespoons (60 ml) olive oil, divided*
*4 whole trout, boned, gutted, head and*
*  fins removed*
*Kosher salt*
*Freshly ground pepper*
*8 (⅛-inch /0.3 cm thick) slices pancetta*
*  (bacon may be substituted)*
*2 tablespoons (30 ml) diced shallots*
*2 tablespoons (30 ml) sherry vinegar*

While vegetables are roasting, peel skins from cooled pearl onions, place in small saucepan, and cover with water. Add a few pats of butter. Turn heat to medium-high and cook until onions are tender and can be pierced with a knife. Add more water as necessary. Once beet is cool, peel and cut into medium dice and place in large bowl. As vegetables are done cooking, add them to bowl. Toss to mix and set aside.

Preheat oven to 350°F (180°C). Heat 2 tablespoons (30 ml) olive oil in large cast-iron skillet over medium-high heat until barely smoking. Season trout inside and out with salt and pepper. Close trout back up and wrap each with 2 pieces of pancetta. Place trout in hot pan and cook for approximately 5 minutes, until golden brown. Flip fish over onto a baking sheet and put in oven for 5 to 6 minutes. Trout is done when a knife inserted into the middle comes out hot. Remove from pan and save in a warm place.

Wipe out the frying pan and reheat on medium-high. Add 1 tablespoon (15 ml) olive oil, and once the pan is hot, add roasted root vegetables. Toss to heat evenly. Cook until they begin to brown slightly. Season with salt and pepper. Transfer to bowl and keep warm.

Return pan to medium-high heat. Add remaining olive oil and shallots and cook for 1 to 2 minutes, making sure shallots don't color. Add vinegar carefully to avoid splashing. Remove from heat and taste for seasoning.

To serve, put some polenta and root vegetables on each plate. Gently lay fish over the top and drizzle with the vinaigrette.

*Chef Colton Soelberg, Sundance Resort, Sundance, Utah*

# Hazelnut Trout

*serves two*

### Hazelnut Flour

*1 cup (135 g) whole roasted hazelnuts*

*½ cup (65 g) all-purpose flour*

*¼ cup (35 g) cornmeal*

*2 tablespoons (25 g) sugar*

*½ teaspoon (1.5 g) garlic powder*

*½ teaspoon (1.2 g) onion powder*

*½ teaspoon (3 g) salt*

*1 teaspoon (1.2 g) chopped rosemary leaves*

### Trout Fillets

*2 rainbow trout, deboned, head and tail removed, and butterflied*

*6 tablespoons (85 g) butter, divided*

*Juice of 1 lemon wedge*

*¼ cup (60 ml) hazelnut liqueur*

*Parsley, chopped*

Place ½ cup (68 g) hazelnuts in food processor and grind to flour consistency. Add flour, cornmeal, sugar, garlic powder, onion powder, and salt to food processor. Pulse a few times to blend with hazelnuts. Transfer to a bowl. Add rosemary to mixture. Place remaining whole hazelnuts in food processor and pulse to a small pea-size consistency. Add to flour mixture.

Wash and gently pat the trout fillets with a paper towel. Do not dry them completely or flour will not adhere to them.

Dredge trout in hazelnut flour, flesh-side down, pressing in some larger bits of hazelnut. Turn over and cover any uncoated areas with hazelnut flour. Heat a large nonstick frying pan over medium heat. Melt 3 tablespoons (42 g) butter. Add trout, skin-side up, when butter begins to bubble. Sauté on medium heat until flour begins to turn golden (approximately 5 minutes). If it smokes, the heat is too high.

Squeeze juice from 1 lemon wedge over trout. Trout will brown more quickly now; wait 10 to 15 seconds and then turn over to skin side. Continue cooking for about 1 minute. To check for doneness, raise trout with a spatula; if trout splits open showing white, flaky flesh, it is cooked. If trout does not split open, even with a helping hand, place back into pan until cooked. Once trout is cooked, remove and place on plate.

Drain and wipe pan of remaining butter and excess flour. Return pan to high heat. Pour in hazelnut liqueur. Remove pan from stove and ignite with a match or lighter. When flames recede, add 3 tablespoons (42 g) butter. Keep pan moving; when sauce becomes thick and bubbly, pour over trout. Lightly sprinkle trout with chopped parsley.

*Chef David Caron, Tall Timber Lodge and Log Cabins, Pittsburg, New Hampshire*

TALL TIMBER LODGE AND LOG CABINS, Pittsburg, New Hampshire

# Highland Salmon

*serves four*

### Highland Salmon Sauce
*1½ cups (355 ml) heavy cream*
*1½ cups (355 ml) orange juice*
*2 tablespoons (12 g) diced green onions*
*2 tablespoons (30 g) brown sugar*
*2 teaspoons (10 g) Dijon mustard*

### Salmon
*4 (6- to 8-ounce/170 to 225 g) skinless*
*    salmon fillets*
*Salt and freshly ground pepper*
*2 tablespoons (30 ml) Drambuie liqueur*

Combine sauce ingredients in a large saucepan. Bring to a boil. Lower to simmer until reduced by one-fourth. Strain into a bowl and reserve.

Season fillets on both sides with salt and pepper. Place salmon fillets on grill and cook for about 2 minutes. Rotate the fillets 90 degrees on the grill to create cross hatched grill marks. Flip salmon over on the grill. Again, rotate after 2 minutes and cook until fish springs back immediately when pressed with a finger. Remove from grill and keep warm until ready to serve.

Preheat grill to medium-high, then coat evenly with cooking spray.

Place ½ cup (120 ml) of sauce in a 10-inch (26 cm) nonstick skillet over medium-high heat until it bubbles. Put the fillets in the pan with the sauce. When the sauce begins to bubble again, pour Drambuie over salmon. Remove pan from heat and ignite the Drambuie with a match or lighter. When flames recede, reduce heat to medium-high. Occasionally shake pan to coat salmon with sauce and to be sure sauce doesn't burn. Continue cooking until sauce darkens and coats the back of a spoon.

Place salmon on platter or individual plates and pour thickened sauce over it.

*Chef David Caron, Tall Timber Lodge and Log Cabins, Pittsburg, New Hampshire*

# Smoked Salmon Pasta with Capers, Roasted Red Peppers, and Parmesan Cheese

*serves two*

1 tablespoon (15 ml) olive oil

1 tablespoon (10 g) minced fresh garlic

1 (6-ounce/170 g) jar or can roasted red peppers, sliced into ribbons

2 tablespoons (17 g) capers, rinsed and drained

Salt and pepper to taste

1 cup (130 g) diced vegetables of your choice

8 ounces (226 g) smoked salmon, crumbled

⅔ cup (160 ml) heavy cream

½ pound (226 g) linguine, cooked al dente

¼ cup (25 g) shredded Parmesan cheese

Heat a large frying pan with olive oil until oil is barely smoking. Sauté garlic, roasted red peppers, capers, salt, pepper, and vegetables for 1½ minutes. Add smoked salmon and sauté for 1 more minute. Mix in heavy cream and bring to a boil. Let cream reduce by about one-third. Toss in pasta and cook for 1 minute more.

Place the smoked salmon pasta in a serving bowl and sprinkle with Parmesan cheese.

**Vermejo Park Ranch, Raton, New Mexico**

Vermejo Park Ranch, Raton, New Mexico

# Baked Salmon with Mustard and Tarragon

*serves four*

4 (6- to 8-ounce/170 to 225 g) salmon
    fillets, skin on

Salt and pepper

½ cup (118 g) mayonnaise

2 tablespoons (30 ml) Dijon mustard

2 tablespoons (8 g) chopped fresh tarragon
    (or 2 teaspoons/3 g dried)

¼ teaspoon (1 ml) white wine vinegar

Lemon wedges

Preheat oven to 350°F (180°C). Place salmon, skin-side down, on ungreased roasting pan. Season with salt and pepper.

Whisk mayonnaise, mustard, tarragon, and vinegar in small bowl to blend; season with salt and pepper. Spread over top and sides of salmon, covering completely. Cover pan tightly with heavy-duty foil. Bake, covered, for 30 minutes. Meanwhile, preheat broiler.

Remove fish from oven. Uncover pan and place under broiler until topping is deep golden brown and salmon feels firm to touch. Serve with lemon wedges.

*Wapiti Meadow Ranch, Cascade, Idaho*

WAPITI MEADOW RANCH,
Cascade, Idaho

# Mustard Seed Crusted Salmon with Mustard Cream Sauce

*serves four*

½ cup (120 ml) dry white wine

¼ cup (40 g) chopped shallots

3 tablespoons (33 g) yellow mustard seeds,
   divided

¾ cup (175 ml) heavy cream

5 tablespoons (75 g) whole-grain Dijon
   mustard, divided

1 tablespoon (4 g) chopped fresh tarragon

Salt and freshly ground black pepper

4 (6- to 8-ounce/170 to 225 g) skinless
   salmon fillets

2 tablespoons (28 g) butter

Preheat oven to 350°F (180°C). Combine wine, shallots, and one-third the mustard seeds in small heavy saucepan set on high and boil until mixture is reduced to ½ cup (120 ml), about 2 minutes. Whisk in cream, half the Dijon mustard, and the tarragon. Boil until thickened to sauce consistency, about 3 minutes. Season with salt and pepper. Remove from heat and cover to keep warm.

Brush salmon on both sides with remaining Dijon mustard. Sprinkle salt, pepper, and remaining mustard seeds on both sides of salmon. Wrap tightly in foil and bake for 30 to 40 minutes. Fish is done when it springs back immediately when pressed with a finger.

Reheat sauce slightly, add butter, and whisk until melted.

To serve, transfer fish to a platter and spoon mustard sauce over the tops.

**Wapiti Meadow Ranch, Cascade, Idaho**

# Cranberry-Glazed Salmon

*serves two*

### Topping

1 tablespoon (15 ml) olive oil

½ cup (80 g) chopped onion

1 tablespoon (20 g) chopped dried shiitake
   mushrooms

1 teaspoon (3 g) minced garlic

¼ cup (38 g) dried cranberries

2 tablespoons (8 g) chopped fresh parsley

2 tablespoons (3.5 g) chopped fresh
   rosemary

½ teaspoon (0.4 g) minced fresh thyme

½ teaspoon (0.4 g) minced fresh sage

Salt and pepper

### Salmon Fillet

2 (6- to 8-ounce/170 to 225 g)
   salmon fillets

¼ cup (69.3 g) canned jellied
   cranberry sauce

Combine all topping ingredients in a bowl and mix well. Season to taste with salt and pepper.

Preheat oven to 350°F (180°C). Coat salmon fillets with cranberry mixture. Wrap tightly in foil and bake for 30 minutes. Open the foil package and check for doneness. Fish is done when it springs back immediately when pressed with a finger. If it's not done, reseal the foil and return it to the oven for another 5 minutes and check again.

To serve, transfer salmon to serving platter or individual plates. Warm cranberry sauce in a small pan until it liquefies and drizzle over salmon.

**Wapiti Meadow Ranch, Cascade, Idaho**

# Pesto-Stuffed Salmon

*serves four*

4 (6- to 8-ounce/170 to 226 g) salmon
  fillets, skin on
1 (4-ounce/115 g) jar basil pesto
Olive oil for brushing
Salt and freshly ground white pepper
  to taste

**Scallop Cream**
½ cup (120 ml) heavy cream
½ cup (115 g) sour cream
1 tablespoon (2.5 g) minced basil
Pinch of freshly grated nutmeg
4 large bay scallops

Preheat oven to 375°F (190°C). Slice a pocket halfway through the surface of each salmon fillet and stuff with pesto. Brush with olive oil and season with salt and white pepper. Bake for 20 minutes.

Combine heavy cream and sour cream in large skillet. Heat and whisk until smooth. Add basil, nutmeg, salt, and pepper to taste, and simmer to reduce and thicken slightly.

In a small pot, bring 3 inches (7.5 cm) of water to a boil. Drop in scallops, reduce to a simmer, and cook, covered, just until opaque (about 3 minutes). Drain and dry scallops and add to hot cream sauce.

Serve immediately by spooning one scallop and some sauce over each salmon fillet. Remaining sauce can be served on the side.

***Wapiti Meadow Ranch, Cascade, Idaho***

# Salmon with Herb Sauce

*serves four*

4 tablespoons (55 g) butter, plus
   1 tablespoon (14 g) for greasing
   baking sheet

1 tablespoon (15 ml) fresh lime juice

1 tablespoon (6 g) freshly grated lime zest

1 teaspoon (1.5 g) Old Bay or other seafood
   seasoning

2 cups (100 g) fresh unflavored
   bread crumbs

2 garlic cloves, minced

½ cup (30 g) chopped parsley

½ cup (20 g) chopped basil

4 (6- to 8-ounce/170 to 225 g) salmon
   fillets, skin on

Salt and pepper to taste

### Herb Sauce

⅓ cup (80 ml) heavy cream

⅓ cup (77 g) sour cream

2 tablespoons (6 g) chopped chives

2 tablespoons (5 g) finely chopped basil

1 tablespoon (4 g) finely chopped parsley

1 teaspoon (5 ml) lemon juice

Preheat oven to 400°F (200°C). Butter a large baking sheet. Melt butter in skillet and stir in lime juice, zest, Old Bay seasoning, bread crumbs, and garlic. Cook mixture, stirring frequently, until bread crumbs are crisp and golden. Remove from heat and stir in parsley and basil.

Season salmon with salt and pepper and coat top with bread crumb mixture. Bake in middle of oven 30 minutes. Check for doneness. Fish is done when it springs back immediately when pressed with a finger. If it's not done, return it to the oven for another few minutes and check again.

In a small bowl, whisk together herb sauce ingredients until smooth. Put sauce on the bottom of a serving platter or individual plates. Place salmon fillets onto sauce and serve.

***Wapiti Meadow Ranch, Cascade, Idaho***

# Grilled Salmon with Citrus and Herbs

*serves four*

2 teaspoons (3.5 g) grated lemon zest
2 teaspoons (3.5 g) grated lime zest
1 tablespoon (10 g) minced garlic
½ teaspoon (1 g) black pepper
1½ teaspoons (9 g) coarse salt
1 tablespoon (15 ml) olive oil
1 tablespoon (2.5 g) chopped thyme
1 tablespoon (4 g) chopped parsley
4 (6- to 8-ounce/170 to 226 g) salmon
   fillets, skin on

Preheat oven to 350°F (180°C). Combine all ingredients, except salmon. Mix well and rub on salmon. Cover tightly with heavy-duty foil and bake for 30 minutes. Open the foil package and check for doneness. Fish is done when it springs back immediately when pressed with a finger. If it's not done, reseal the foil and return it to the oven for another 5 minutes and check again.

To serve, transfer fillets to serving platter or individual plates. Spoon juices accumulated on the bottom of the foil over the fillets.

**Wapiti Meadow Ranch, Cascade, Idaho**

# Fishing Lodges Directory

Here is a listing of all of the destinations we have included in our book. We encourage you to take a few minutes to visit their Web sites for a more complete look at their offerings, facilities, and dining experiences.

## Baranof Wilderness Lodge

Mike Trotter, owner and operator of Baranof Wilderness Lodge and Beyond Boundaries Expeditions, has more than twenty-two years of outfitting, exploring, and fishing experience to give his guests the ultimate in Alaskan wilderness and fishing experience. Located 20 miles (32 km) east of Sitka and nestled in Warm Springs Bay on the east side of Baranof Island, the Baranof Wilderness Lodge offers abundant and diverse saltwater and freshwater fishing. Dozens of spectacular bays, estuaries, fishing streams, and lakes are within a short boat ride or hike from the lodge.

**P.O. Box 2187**
**Sitka, Alaska  99835**
**1.800.613.6551**
**www.flyfishalaska.com**

## Big Hole C4 Lodge

Nestled in 400 acres (160 ha) of picturesque Montana terrain and surrounded by 20 miles (32 km) of private waters is the Big Hole C4 Lodge. This remote setting provides a true Montana fly-fishing experience, offering the biggest brown and rainbow trout around.

**80 Ultley Lane**
**Twin Bridges, Montana  59754**
**1.877.684.5760**
**www.bigholec4lodge.com**

## Blackberry Farm

Named the 2003 and 2004 Orvis-Endorsed Lodge of the Year, this beautiful farm sits on 4,200 acres (1680 ha) in the Great Smoky Mountains and offers the best fly-fishing east of the Rocky Mountains. Guides and instructors are available. There are two ponds and a stream on the property and more than 700 miles (1100 km) of fishable trout streams in the neighboring Great Smoky Mountain National Park and Clinch River.

**1471 West Millers Cove Road**
**Walland, Tennessee  37886**
**800.648.4252**
**www.blackberryfarm.com**

## The Lodge and Ranch at Chama Land and Cattle Company

From tiny rivulets to spring creeks to high canyon rivers and over a dozen lakes that hold browns, brookies, rainbows, and cutthroats, Chama offers a fishing experience for every level of fisherman. The 27,000-square-foot (24000 sq m) Lodge at Chama surrounded by 36,000 acres (14000 ha) offers world-class facilities and cuisine.

**P.O. Box 127**
**Chama, New Mexico  87520**
**505.756.2133**
**www.lodgeatchama.com**

## Clayoquot Wilderness Resorts

Clayoquot Sound is home to the largest wild steelhead population in the world, and resort guides know all the hot spots. Fly-fish for spring steelhead, fall salmon, or cutthroat trout throughout the sound's extensive river system. From May through September, find coho (silver salmon) and sea bass; in the summer, giant tyee (king salmon); and March through September prolific deep-sea halibut. Clayoquot river systems percolate with winter and spring steelhead and sea-run cutthroat trout. Prime fly and spinning seasons vary with spring hatches and water levels. Experienced guides ensure productive outings. The resort has sport-fishing vessels with state-of-the-art electronics and navigational equipment. The Wilderness Outpost at Bedwell River offers guests luxurious white canvas deluxe guest and family suite tents, plus dining tents, spa tents, and lounge. This flagship property and the floating property at Quait Bay both offer adventure and genteel luxury.

**Box 130**
**Tofino, British Columbia, Canada**
**888.333.5405**
**www.wildretreat.com**

## Clearwater Lodge on the Pit River

The Clearwater Lodge on the Pit River is housed in a magnificent Arts and Crafts building completed in 1921. Using lava rock and clear fir from the surrounding forests, skilled craftsmen created a masterwork of lodge architecture unique in California. Located in a parklike setting on the Pit River, this unusual full-service fly-fishing destination offers meals and accommodations as well as guiding through and instruction on northeastern California's five great wild trout rivers and spring-fed still waters.

**24500 Pit One Powerhouse Road**
**Fall River Mills, California 96028**
**530.336.5005**
**www.clearwaterlodge.com**

## Crescent H Ranch in Jackson Hole

With miles of private spring creeks, trout-filled ponds, and the magnificent Snake River, the fabled fisheries of the Ranch and Jackson Hole area continue to beckon fly-fishers. You can choose a dawn-to-dusk regimen of Rocky Mountain activities or a slower-paced schedule complete with spa amenities for your stay.

**P.O. Box 347**
**Wilson, Wyoming 83014**
**307.732.0784**
**www.crescenthranch.com**

## Eldred Preserve

Known as Sullivan County's premier fishing resort, this year-round outdoor resort is a short drive from Metro New York, New Jersey, and Pennsylvania. Set on 3,000 acres (1200 ha), it caters to fishing and shooting enthusiasts providing fine food, drink, and lodging accommodations.

**1040 Rte. 55**
**P.O. Box 111**
**Eldred, NY 12732**
**845.557.8316 or 800.557.FISH**
**www.eldredpreserve.com**

## Elk Lake Lodge

Elk Lake is the centerpiece of a 12,000-acre (4800 ha) privately owned forest preserve in the heart of the High Peaks region. Boating and fishing are offered on the 600-acre (240 ha) Elk Lake, with its open water, inlets, bays, and many islands, as well as on the 200-acre (80 ha) deep glacial waters of Clear Pond. Speckled trout are available at Elk Lake and lake trout and landlocked salmon at Clear Pond through periodic stocking programs. Fly-fishing takes place in any of several rushing streams and mountain ponds.

**County Road 84**
**North Hudson, NY 12855**
**518.532.7616**
**www.elklakelodge.com**

## Favorite Bay Lodge

Both saltwater and freshwater fishing experiences are available at Favorite Bay Lodge. Local guides, all Coast Guard certified, have been fishing these waters their entire lives and provide everything you need to catch "the big one." In minutes, guests can travel by small boat to the mouth of native streams healthy with runs of Dolly Varden, cutthroat, and steelhead trout. All five species of wild Pacific salmon, monster halibut, and a fabulous variety of rockfish are available, as well as seasonal freshwater salmon. Guests can fish these streams from shore, kayak, or canoe, and follow them to hidden lakes that are their source. Experienced native guides will assist all levels of anglers with fly rod and ultra-light spinning gear.

**P.O. Box 149**
**Angoon, Alaska  99820**
**866.788.3344**
**www.favoritebaylodge.com**

## Flying B Ranch

This Orvis-endorsed fly-fishing lodge is strategically located near the Clearwater River. As a nationally recognized steelhead fishery, Flying B Ranch offers guests access to over seventy miles of this pristine water. The Flying B Ranch caters to the steelhead fisherman whose desire is the thrill of landing that 12- to 22-pound (5.44 to 9.97 kg) steelhead trout with a fly. Power and drift boats equipped with bait and spinning tackle are available.

**2900 Lawyer Creek Road**
**Kamiah, Idaho  83536**
**800.472.1945**
**208.935.0755**
**www.flyingbranch.com**

## Gaston's White River Resort

This resort is home to world-renowned fishing for brown and rainbow trout. Most people come to Gaston's for breathtaking scenery and trophy-sized trout, but guests can also find year-round diversions for the entire family.

**1777 River Road**
**Lakeview, Arkansas  72642**
**870.431.5202**

**www.gastons.com**

## Great Alaska Adventure Lodge

Whether you are a seasoned fly angler or first-time spin fisherman, the variety of experience, volume of fish, and available round-the-clock fishing assure guests of an excellent fishing trip. This Orvis-endorsed lodge specializes in providing guests with bountiful salmon, trout, and halibut fishing; Alaskan wildlife safaris; and exhilarating wilderness activities.

*Winter* **(September 22 to April 22)**
**P.O. Box 2670**
**Poulsbo, Washington  98370**
**360.697.6454**

*Summer*
**33881 Sterling Highway**
**Sterling, Alaska  99672**
**907.262.4515**
**www.greatalaska.com**

## Grosse Savanne Waterfowl and Wildlife Lodge

Located in the southwest corner of Louisiana, Grosse Savanne is  nestled in the heart of Cameron Parish County and provides easy access to abundant wildlife and fisheries as well as freshwater and saltwater marshes. Grosse Savanne encompasses more than 50,000 acres (20000 ha) of wetlands, prairies, and agricultural fields, and it is bordered by the finest saltwater lake in the state—all providing abundant opportunities for visiting sportsmen.

**1730 Big Pasture Road**
**Lake Charles, Louisiana  70607**
**337.598.2357**
**www.grossesavanne.com**

## Hawk's Cay Resort

This 60-acre (24 ha) resort and spa is in the heart of the Florida Keys and is a little piece of paradise for all kinds of outdoor enthusiasts, including those with a passion for reeling in their catch.

**61 Hawk's Cay Boulevard**
**Duck Key, Florida 33050**
**888.443.6393 or 305.743.7000**
**www.hawkscay.com**

## Henry's Fork Lodge

This lodge was built at the heart of the country's finest fly-fishing. The rivers contain only wild fish, not hatchery stockers, making every outing a genuine fly-fishing experience. Anglers worldwide have called Henry's Fork the finest dry-fly stream in the world. In addition to Henry's Fork, the area boasts an honor roll of great fly-fishing rivers, including the Madison, Gallatin, and Yellowstone.

**2794 South Pinehaven Drive**
**Island Park, Idaho 83429**
**208.558.7953**
**www.henrysforklodge.com**

## Highland Ranch

The Highland Ranch has been run by the Gaines family since 1987, and they pride themselves on running a friendly, casual place in an unhurried environment. The spectacular setting is a fisherman's paradise. Highland Lake teems with largemouth bass, bluegills, crappies, and catfish—just the right mix to keep even the most experienced angler challenged. There is also a smaller pond where the kids can enjoy fishing. No need to bring fishing gear from home; it's all here, along with bait and shovels. The ranch will also clean and cook your fish for you.

**P.O. Box 150**
**Philo, California 95466**
**707.895.3600**
**www.highlandranch.com**

## The Homestead

Nestled in Virginia's Allegheny Mountains, the Homestead is one of Virginia's premier mountain resorts and a National Historic Landmark. In operation since 1766, it offers great fly-fishing. Orvis-endorsed, there is trout fishing, a fly-fishing school, and a children's fishing pond.

**1766 Homestead Drive**
**Hot Springs, Virginia 24445**
**866.354.4653**
**www.thehomestead.com**

## Keyah Grande

Husband-and-wife team Barbara and Alan Sackman own this 4,000-acre (1600 ha) luxury retreat in southwestern Colorado that caters to nature lovers. Among the array of outdoor activities is catch-and-release fly- and cast-fishing, and there are guided river fishing tours in season.

**13211 Highway 160 West**
**Pagosa Springs, Colorado 81147**
**970.731.1160**
**www.keyahgrande.com**

## Libby Camps, Sporting Lodges and Outfitter

This Orvis-endorsed catch-and-release lodge in Maine has been operating for over 100 years, with the Libby family at the helm for five generations. Fly-fishing and spin-fishing vacations for Maine brook trout, landlocked salmon, lakers, and bass are said to be the finest in the East. Eight simple cabins, handcrafted from peeled spruce and fir logs, lit by kerosene lamps and heated by woodstoves, are situated just back from the water. Exceptional Maine guides are available, as are home-cooked family style meals. Lodge seaplanes access ten outpost camps, and there are eighty canoes and boats on over thirty different waters within a 20-mile

(32 km) radius of camp. The camps are 45 miles (70 km) from the nearest town by private gravel road.

**P.O. Box 810**
**Ashland, Maine 04732**
**207.435.8274**
**www.libbycamps.com**

**The Lodge on Little St. Simons Island**
Recognized for its untouched natural beauty, Little St. Simons Island, a private island rental and island getaway, lies just off the Georgia coast. Accessible only by boat, this private island offers 10,000 perfectly preserved wilderness acres (4000 ha) with access to redfish, sea trout, and other valued game species. Experience light spinning, surfcasting, saltwater, and freshwater fly-fishing as well as conventional angling. Gear, bait, and advice are complimentary. Peak fishing runs from mid-August through early December, when the marshes are at the height of productivity, and reds and sea trout eagerly await the crop of shrimp, crabs, and baitfish. The centerpiece of the island's fly-fishing is three small tidal creeks that empty into the Atlantic Ocean. Nearly impossible to navigate by boat, island guests get exclusive land-based access to fish these isolated waters. There are 7 miles (11 km) of shell-strewn beaches enjoyed by no more than thirty overnight guests at a time.

**P. O. Box 21078**
**1000 Hampton Point Drive**
**Little St. Simons Island, Georgia 31522**
**888.733.5774**
**912.638.7472**
**www.LittleStSimonsIsland.com**

**Nimmo Bay**
For over twenty-six years, the Murray family has specialized in world-class hospitality. Listed in the book *1000 Places to See Before You Die*, Nimmo Bay Resort is a luxurious high-end helicopter fly-fishing and helicopter adventure destination nestled at the foot of Mount Stevens along the Great Bear Rainforest coastline. Guests depart the resort each morning in A-Star helicopters and travel from sea level to 7,000 feet (2000 m) and down again into the Great Bear Rainforest, where some of the most private and desirable freshwater fishing in the world awaits. Fly-fish or spin-fish all day for rainbow trout, steelhead, char, and all five species of Pacific salmon: chinook, coho, chum, sockeye, and pink.

**P.O. Box 696**
**Port McNeill, British Columbia**
**V0N 2R0**
**800.837.HELI or 250.956.4000**
**www.nimmobay.com**

**North Knife Lake Lodge**
Hosts Mike and Jeanne Reimer and Nelson and Toni Morberg have lived and operated here for the last thirty-five years. Known as one of Manitoba's most unique, diverse, and exclusive fly-in fishing destinations, North Knife's main body of water holds trophy northern pike and lake trout. Arctic grayling also inhabit a few of the in- and out-flowing rivers. Only sixteen guests experience this "one of a kind" fishery each trip. Guests have caught and released northern pike up to 52.5 inches (133.35 cm), lake trout up to 47 inches (119.38 cm), and arctic grayling up to 22.5 inches (57.15 cm). Professional guides maximize angling opportunities. North Knife Lake Lodge also offers a wide variety of daily fly-outs to add to this unique fishing experience.

**P. O. Box 425**
**Thompson, Manitoba, Canada R8N 1N2**
**1.888.WEBBERS**
**www.webberslodges.com**

### The Inn at Palmetto Bluff

This peaceful, pampering retreat is the newest addition to world-renowned Auberge Resorts. Just minutes from Savannah and Hilton Head Island, it is situated in the picturesque South Carolina Low Country along the beautiful May River. Families can enjoy crabbing and shrimping and fishermen can spin- or fly-fish, go deep-sea fishing on a yacht, or kayak fish with a guide.

**476 Mount Pelia Road**
**Bluffton, South Carolina 29910**
**843.706.6500**
**www.palmettobluffresort.com**

### Rainbow Ranch Lodge

Located in the heart of the Rocky Mountains in southwest Montana, the Rainbow Ranch Lodge and Big Sky/Yellowstone area offer world class fly-fishing. Guests can literally cast a line off their back deck into the Gallatin River or join a guide for a casting clinic, half-day or full-day walk/wade trip, full day float trip, or horseback ride to a wilderness alpine lake.

**PO 160336**
**Big Sky, Montana 59716**
**800.937.4132**

### The Resort at Paws Up

Paws Up is a 37,000-acre (15000 ha) ranch nestled in the foothills of the Garnet Mountains in the heart of the Blackfoot Valley in Montana. The 7 scenic miles (11 km) of the Big Blackfoot River that wind through Paws Up offer some of the best fly-fishing in the West. With over six species of game fish, the "Big Blackie" has much variety for the avid angler. The Blackfoot has gained recognition worldwide due to its prominence in the best-selling novel *A River Runs Through It* by Norman Maclean and the successful movie directed by Robert Redford and starring Brad Pitt.

**40060 Paws Up Road**
**Greenough, Montana 59823**
**406.244.5200**
**866.894.7969**
**www.pawsup.com**

### Rough Creek Lodge and Resort

There's no roughing it at Rough Creek, which boasts a long list of awards, including being named Most Outstanding Lodge in America by Condé Nast Johansens and one of America's Top Restaurants for three years in a row by Zagat. This luxury resort in Texas offers dockside fishing, fishing instruction, and guided fishing trips where you can catch bass, perch, crappie, and catfish on numerous lakes.

**5165 County Road 2013**
**Glen Rose, Texas 76043**
**800.864.4705**
**www.roughcreek.com**

### Siwash Lake Ranch

Surrounded by 80,000 acres (32000 ha) of pristine British Columbia wilderness, Siwash Lake Ranch offers all types of fishing, from traditional shoreline spin-casting to trolling from a boat to fly-fishing. The Cariboo region's rivers, lakes, and streams provide spawning, rearing, and foraging habitat for wild native fish, including BC's legendary rainbow trout. Prolific fly hatches, a nutrient-rich environment, and clear, cold waters make this area a fantastic fishing destination. There are more than nine excellent trout-fishing lakes and a river close by. Personal angling guides take guests to favorite fishing spots in the ranch's four-wheel-drive truck.

**P. O. Box 39**
**70 Mile House**
**British Columbia, Canada V0K2K0**
**250.395.6541**
**www.siwashlakeranch.com**

### Snake River Lodge & Spa

Snake River took the AAA Four Diamond Award in 2007 for lodging, was honored by readers of Condé Nast Traveler as one of the Top Ten Resorts in the United States in 2004, and was voted to their Gold List in 2005. There is an in-house fly-fishing school with casting lessons, fly-tying lessons and demonstrations, and guided trips on local rivers like the Snake. Both beginners and experienced anglers are welcome.

**P.O. Box 348**
**7710 Granite Loop Road**
**Teton Village, Wyoming  83025**
**866.975.ROCK or 307.732.6000**
**www.snakeriverlodge.rockresorts.com**

### Spotted Horse Ranch

The runoff from nearly 400 inches (1000 cm) of snow each winter provides Jackson Hole with some of the best streams and rivers for spawning and growing trout. Snake River fine-spotted cutthroat, rainbow, and brown trout thrive in the cool waters. Vigorous and hungry, they offer virtually every level of fly caster a satisfying experience. A new addition to this Orvis-endorsed ranch is a spring-fed pond with its very own cutthroat population to help anglers build confidence and improve casting skills. From there, guests can work their way to fishing the Hoback and Willow Creek on the ranch, or take a guided fishing trip on the Snake or Green rivers. "The Trout School" at the ranch is a must for beginners and intermediates.

**12355 S Hwy. 191**
**Jackson Hole, Wyoming  83001**
**800.528.2084**
**307.733.2097**
**www.spottedhorseranch.com**

### Spring Lake Hunting Lodge and Resort

South Dakota contains some of the finest fishing waters in North America. Between the mountain lakes and streams of the Black Hills and the glacial lakes of eastern South Dakota, anglers will find fishing opportunities in stock dams, prairie rivers, and giant reservoirs. Nearly thirty fish species provide anglers with a variety of fishing adventures. The most popular fish include walleye, perch, bass, and pike. South Dakota's fishing season is open almost year-round, providing quality, four-season fishing.

Within ten minutes of the lodge are four lakes (Lake Thompson, Lake Sinai, Twin Lakes on 81, and Lake Whitewood) with some of the finest walleye, perch, and pike fishing in South Dakota.

**44915 218th St.**
**Oldham, South Dakota  57051**
**605.482.9663**
**www.springlakehuntinglodgeandresort.com**

### Sundance Resort

In 1969, Robert Redford bought Timphaven, then a local ski resort, along with its surrounding land, and Sundance was born. This renowned resort is an Orvis-endorsed fly-fishing lodge where guests can cast their lines in one of the Provo River's perfect hideouts to try to outsmart a few rainbow, cutthroat, and German brown trout.

**RR3 Box A-1**
**Sundance, Utah  84604**
**801.225.4107**
**www.sundanceresort.com**

## Tall Timber Lodge and Log Cabins

Tall Timber Lodge is a relaxed and rustic resort made for outdoorsmen. It has received numerous kudos, including four years straight as Editor's Pick in *Yankee* magazine's Travel Guide to New England. Located in the heart of northern New Hampshire's unspoiled wilderness, it offers unparalleled fishing, canoeing, kayaking, hunting, and moose watching!

**609 Beach Road**
**Pittsburg, New Hampshire  03592**
**800.83LODGE**
**www.talltimber.com**

## Vermejo Ranch

The creation of Ted Turner, Vermejo is paradise for the outdoorsman, but especially for the fisherman. There are twenty-one well-stocked lakes providing rainbow, brown, brook, and cutthroat trout, most of which average 1 to 2 pounds (0.45 to 0.9 kg). Stream-fishing enthusiasts will find some 30 miles (48 km) of small to medium streams traversing Vermejo with brook, rainbow, and cutthroat trout. In addition, Vermejo's streams offer one of the few remaining places inhabited by the Rio Grande cutthroat. The ranch's fishing season runs from late May to mid-September. Optimum stream flow usually starts in late June or early July. While late May weather may be unpredictable, the lake fishing is superb for subsurface patterns. Late June and July produce regular hatches of caddis, damselflies, and mayflies, sending trout into feeding frenzies.

**P.O. Drawer E**
**Raton, NM  87740**
**505.445.3097**
**www.vermejoparkranch.com**

## Wapiti Meadow Ranch

This Orvis-endorsed ranch is adjacent to the largest wilderness area in the continental United States. With over 50 miles (80 km) of freestone stream fishing in and adjacent to the largest wilderness area in the Lower 48, Wapiti Meadow offers fly enthusiasts the best in wade fishing on the headwaters of the legendary Salmon River system, including the blue-ribbon cutthroat waters of the mighty Middle Fork. Nine lakes accessed by horseback, foot, or 4x4 trails provide opportunities to enjoy the alpine reaches of the spectacular Salmon River Mountains, as well as its stream valleys. Many streams and high mountain lakes ensure fly-fishing variety. These and most other lakes are day-trips from the ranch. Wapiti also offers "some deep in the River of No Return Wilderness" fishing that is accessed by horseback and camping. There is also a pond with brook trout.

**1667 Johnson Creek Road**
**Cascade, Idaho  83611**
**208.633.3217**
**www.wapitimeadowranch.com**

# Index

# Photo Credits

Cover: (center) Yvette Cardozo

Page 10 (second from top) Everett Olmstead negative
   no. 9305-A4562, HistoricPhotoArchive.com,
   Portland, OR

Page 11 Baranof Wilderness Lodge Team

Page 21 Courtesy of Big Hole C4 Lodge

Page 22 Courtesy of Blackberry Farm

Page 26 Courtesy of  Lodge at Chama

Page 27 Courtesy of Clayoquot Winderness Resorts

Page 30 S.L. Barson

Page 35 Courtesy of Crescent H Ranch

Page 38 Lou Monteleone

Page 44 Courtesy of Elk Lake Lodge

Page 47 Courtesy of Favorite Bay Lodge

Page 51 Courtesy of Flying B Ranch

Page 57 Debra Edwards John

Page 61 Courtesy of Grosse Savanne Lodge

Page 62 Courtesy of Hawk's Cay Resort, Florida Keys

Page 64 Val Atkinson

Page 66 Courtesy of Highland Guest Ranch

Page 69 Courtesy of The Homestead

Page 73 Courtesy of Libby's Sports Lodges

Page 75 Courtesy of Little St. Simon Island

Page 80 Yvette Cardozo

Page 81 Courtesy of North Knife Lake Lodge

Page 85 Courtesy of Palmetto Bluff

Page 87 Kelly Gorham

Page 90 Courtesy of Rough Creek Lodge & Resort

Page 95 Courtesy of Siwash Lake Ranch

Page 96 Courtesy of Snake River Lodge and Spa

Page 97 Courtesy of Spotted Horse Ranch Inc.

Page 100 Courtesy of Spring Lake Hunting Lodge

Page 101 Courtesy of Sundance Resort

Page 104 Mickey Deneher

Page 107 Courtesy of Vermejo Park Ranch

Page 108 Courtesy of Wapiti Meadow Ranch